The
Wisdom
of
Wealth

MOSAICA PRESS

כתר

בינה   חכמה

גבורה   חסד

תפארת

הוד   נצח

יסוד

מלכות

The
Wisdom
of
Wealth

Torah
Values
Regarding
Money

Chananel Herbsman

Mosaica Press, Inc.
© 2017 by Mosaica Press
Designed and typeset by Brocha Mirel Strizower

Published and distributed by:
Mosaica Press, Inc.
www.mosaicapress.com
info@mosaicapress.com

Rabbi Hershel Schachter
24 Bennett Avenue
New York, New York 10033
(212) 795-0630

הרב צבי שכטר
ראש ישיבה וראש כולל
ישיבת רבינו יצחק אלחנן

— מכתב ברכה —

כבוד ידידי – וידידו דכ"ר הגאון הי"ו אוכ"ר
י"ע גב אבר פנים רבות כתב ידידני. יש
אצלי את מקצת מאורעות ספרי הלז,
וענוניא מכ' מר שקימאות, ולא מ' כון
סמוכ ל, וכן לידב"ר שותפקא הם ספ א
הקבור התורני ספני, ואחנו ומאו
אל הרב זול וזל איב אבא האבתמו
או שא. דוד
הכיותר ורחמש אבא ואבי האבתמו
אא ע שי
אלחן האל

Rabbi Yehuda Parnes
1440 54th Street
Brooklyn, N.Y. 11219

רב יהודה פרנס
ברוקלין, נוא יארק

18 Adar 5777

I would like to express my satisfaction and happiness on seeing my devoted *talmid*, Chananel Herbsman, sharing some of his efforts in Torah with the publication of this *sefer*, *The Wisdom of Wealth*, Chananel is someone I consider a *talmid chaver*. After attending *shiurim* for a number of years, we began to learn *b'chavrusa* which lasted 12 years. He has been an example I used for my students as a model of *yiras shamayim* and dedicated Torah learning despite the burden of *parnasah*.

While I was unable to read the entire manuscript, Chananel has always done thorough research and works with diligence to understand *Chazal* and *Rishonim*. I am confident he has done that here as well. His keen understanding of topics and his exhaustive research will not suprisingly leave the reader of his work with much to think about and grow from in *avodas Hashem*.

I wish him success in spreading *da'as Hashem*.

Sincerely,

yehuda Parnes

Yehuda Parnes

לזכר נשמות הורינו היקרים

הרב שמואל זאב בן ר׳ משה ז״ל
ומרת מאטל בת ר׳ אברהם ע״ה
שטראלי

הרב משה בן ר׳ דוד בנימין ז״ל
ואשתו מרת חנה מרים בת ר׳ יעקב ע״ה
גארפינקעל

אברהם משה
וגאלדה דבורה שטראלי

תנצב״ה

Table of Contents

Acknowledgments

To my wife — I want to express my deep gratitude for all of her support in the process of publishing this book. From the initial idea to the finished product, her encouragement has provided me with the strength to see it through to the end.

To my *rebbe* — there is a great treasury of wisdom that can be found throughout classic rabbinic writings; some of this wisdom is readily available, but much of it requires digging beneath the surface to glean its pearls. I want to thank my *rebbe*, Rabbi Yehudah Parnes, for opening this treasure chest to me and providing me with the tools to dig deep. I am forever grateful for this.

To my parents — I appreciate their life-long support and encouragement. In particular, I thank my mother for teaching and instilling in me at a young age how to utilize time. This was very useful in all phases of preparing and publishing this book.

A number of people read different parts of my original notes and manuscript at various stages, and I thank them for all of their help. Their input helped make this a reality. In particular, I want to thank all of the people at Mosaica Press for their assistance in bringing this project to fruition.

I would be remiss to express my gratitude to the Almighty for giving me the opportunity, ability, and desire to delve into His Torah and to write this book.

Chananel Herbsman

Introduction

In his classic work, *Chovos HaLevavos* (*Duties of the Heart*), Rabbeinu Bachya Ibn Paquda (eleventh-century Spain) describes a society that had lost its way regarding its approach to wealth and physical pleasure:

> *The instinct attracts them to an indulgent lifestyle and a pursuit of wealth, enamoring them of this world's luxury and prominence, until finally they sink in the depths of its sea, forced to face the crush of its waves...The demands of a growing addiction and the pressures of a debilitating materialism preoccupy their minds incessantly with ever-new worldly distractions, entrenching this world's strivings in their hearts... They develop this world at the expense of their minds; the more the world is developed, the more their minds are wasted, until finally they consider the evil way of the world good, the crooked way straight. They even make it the rule and ideal. Parents bequeath [these values] to their children, raising their offspring by them...Their homes are filled with emptiness. What used to be considered strange in the world seems acceptable to them, and the right way appears foreign to them. To be content without luxuries is considered a failure of duty...He who takes from this world only what is sufficient for his needs is called an idler; he who neglects to increase his holdings is considered derelict. One who is content with an adequate livelihood is thought weak; one who is wholly engrossed in worldly gain is thought industrious.[1]*

Material prosperity became so important, the *Chovos HaLevavos* continues, that "they made their bellies their god, their clothing their religion, improvement of their dwellings their ideal."

If this occurred nearly one thousand years ago, then it certainly could happen today in a world that has much greater material wealth than in ages gone by! In fact, how can a person be sure that this hasn't

> *They develop this world at the expense of their minds.*

already taken place? How does someone evaluate whether he is on a good "path" or has veered from it?

The realm of wealth and money can be somewhat deceptive, as indicated in the *Chovos HaLevavos*. A person might think he is doing all the right things, while in actuality he is far off course. Failing to have the proper perspective on wealth can occur even in the best of times.

Today, it is even more challenging to obtain a clear perspective on wealth because the environment in which we live (the wealthiest society in the history of mankind) creates confusion in our minds about how to evaluate wealth. On a daily ba-

> *The realm of money can be deceptive.*

sis, we are bombarded by advertisements in varying forms of media that beckon us to pursue all we can possibly desire, conveying the message that we absolutely need more, and that indulgence is the proper path.

Advertisements present the possibility of a beautiful world full of pleasure, enjoyment, and the implicit promise of happiness. Credit cards have made it easy to purchase products even if we don't have the money for them. The combination of easy access to making purchases and the continuous message projected through media is a powerful force, one difficult not to succumb to.

Furthermore, we live in a free society in which Jews are able to participate in all aspects of life. During the past fifty years, opportunities have opened up for Jews (Orthodox Jews in particular) that have never existed before. In the past, participation of Jews in certain professions, academia, corporate America, and Wall Street was limited due to religious discrimination. Today, however, although some challenges remain, it is common to find observant Jews filling positions in a wide array of those fields.

In many ways, the world today is entirely different than the world of our grandparents. The options and possibilities for earning a livelihood are almost without limit; for the most part, issues of race and religion are much less significant than ever before. Technology has also changed the world in numerous ways. The Internet has created a new way of conducting business. One of its benefits is that, to a large extent, the online world takes race and religion out of the process. The store is seen through the website, and we don't see the people who own and run it.

Most of these changes have been positive. Still, while change offers opportunities, it also creates new challenges. Because Jewish life is no longer as insular as it once was, ideas from outside the Jewish tradition are more likely to have influence. Sometimes this influence is readily apparent; at other times, such as in the area of wealth (where the Torah's framework is not as obviously structured), it is less apparent. When the parameters of the Torah are not as evident, it is more difficult for a person to sense that ideas are coming from without and that they might not reflect Torah values.

> *Outside influence is very dangerous in the area of wealth, where the Torah's framework is not always structured or self-evident.*

Consequently, the individual is left exposed to elements of the world around him — ideas and values — with very little defense.

It is somewhat perplexing that there is little protection from this erosion of values in the area of wealth. After all, while there has been a great deal of economic growth in the Jewish community, there has also been tremendous growth in Torah study. The Torah itself should serve as a protection by providing guidance in the realm of wealth. However, despite the increasing challenges posed by wealth and the increased study of the Torah, the Torah's teachings regarding wealth receive little attention. Personal finance is not studied formally in school, and the fact that the relevant sources are scattered throughout Scripture and the Talmud make it a difficult topic to study on an individual level. As a result, when young people leave the confines of their schools and enter the workforce, they have little understanding of the proper Jewish attitude toward earning money and acquiring wealth.

Confounding this problem is a lack of parent-guided education concerning finance. In previous generations, even when formal education took place in school, the home was an important forum for education about life. Today, the world is vastly different than it was in the past. Most people work outside their homes, and even when a parent is able to work from home the situation does not usually lend itself to the participation of children. Online businesses and the like are different than running a store from home or across the street. Furthermore, children today have long days in school, so their schedules often preclude them from participating in a family business even when this opportunity is available. Consequently, opportunities for informal financial education are limited. By the time issues of money and wealth become relevant in the lives of young people, many have already left home

There is little opportunity for education in this area.

to study or live on their own. Consequently, even when parents have a proper understanding of the Torah's perspective on wealth, it is often challenging to pass the teaching on to the next generation. This leaves young adults ill-prepared to confront a changing world that offers a different value system than that of the Torah. They are thus left with little protection from the world's ideas and values that may confront them.

The choices people make reflect their values. For a Jew, choices should mirror the values promoted by the Torah and by our Sages, who have transmitted the Torah's teachings. Ultimately, the best weapon in meeting the challenges in the realm of wealth is the Torah; we need to look at the sources and see what the Torah and the Sages teach. It is my hope that this book will make a small contribution in this direction.

While a large part of this book is about understanding the words of Tanach and the teachings of the Sages as presented in classic texts, the wisdom of the Sages is not intended to remain academic. The Sages themselves taught that "study is not primary, but rather action."[2]

Interestingly, sometimes the action called for is development of proper attitudes. Ultimately, actions are determined by beliefs and values, which is why it is essential that a person inculcate within himself the values that come from the ultimate source of truth.

With that said, a word of caution is in order. The reader will obviously notice that this is not a long work. This book will present the basic topics in the area of money and wealth such as financial independence, mitzvos and wealth, and financial planning, but it is by no means encyclopedic, nor can it discuss all views that have been written on a particular subject matter. This book presents the fundamental principles of each topic with most of the basic sources found in early rabbinic literature. Since practical application of principles may involve harmonizing multiple, conflicting principles along with circumstantial constraints, this book is not a how-to book or a practical guide. Rather, it is a presentation of the fundamental concepts regarding wealth in the Torah. Further study, thought, pragmatic evaluation, and perhaps even additional rabbinic insight are necessary when applying these concepts, as their application in the real world is not always straightforward. In certain situations, such as planning for retirement, investing, and other areas of finance, professional financial advice is usually in order as well. It is my hope that this book will help clarify the Torah's positions as they relates to our interaction with wealth and engage readers to delve deeper and see how these ideas can be applied in their own lives.

> *Sometimes, the actions we are called to perform is the development of proper attitudes.*

Part I

The Importance of
Financial Self-Sufficiency

Financial self-sufficiency is at the core of what the Sages teach regarding money and wealth. The phrase, "And don't be in need of other people,"[1] which encapsulates this principle and highlights its importance in daily life, can be found in many places in rabbinic literature. Its impact and practical ramifications can be felt in a wide range of topics. Several theories are presented in this book as to why the Sages felt financial self-sufficiency to be a core value. Following the theories are a number of applications of financial self-sufficiency presented by the Sages. The applications are important as they demonstrate how this fundamental concept impacts other areas of life, such as personal honor and interaction with other people. Ultimately, financial self-sufficiency is not about money; it is about living life with an approach to money that enables a person to meet life's challenges without compromising on his values and his personal relationship with G-d due to monetary dilemmas.

After establishing the basic principle of financial self-sufficiency and looking at its role and impact on other precepts of the Torah, it is necessary to look in particular

Ultimately, financial self-sufficiency is not about money.

at the relationship between financial self-sufficiency and the importance of Torah study. Without question, the need to find a means of financial sufficiency creates a tension with the fundamental commandment to study Torah. The tension between these two principles existed as much in ancient times as it does today. Achieving excellence and mastery in Torah requires a great deal of time and energy. In fact, it is a lifelong pursuit. Torah is not only for the young to study in school; adults and older men continue to study and meditate on its teachings into their old age. With the need to dedicate so much time to the study of Torah, it is obvious that a conflict can arise between the pursuit of financial independence and the pursuit of serious Torah study. The Sages, well aware of this tension, established principles that can be applied to this dilemma. A person interested in pursuing Torah in a serious manner while maintaining his financial self-sufficiency needs to understand these teachings and then apply them to his own circumstances.

Therefore, this section will discuss the conflict between engaging in a livelihood to achieve and maintain financial sufficiency and pursuing the study of Torah in a serious manner.

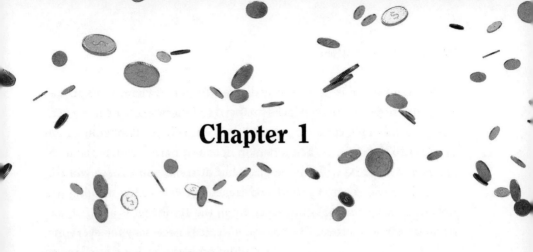

Chapter 1

Fundamentals of
Financial Self-Sufficiency

Numerous sources in Scripture and in the words of the Sages indicate the importance of maintaining financial self-sufficiency. Why is such great emphasis and significance placed on this? Among other things, Scripture and the Sages teach that attaining financial self-sufficiency

- protects from sin;
- helps build a relationship with G-d;
- offers a way to live life to its fullest.

Protection from Sin

"Good is Torah along with work, as toiling at both prevents sin. All Torah that is not accompanied by work will not endure and will lead to sin." (Avos 2:2)

According to one approach, the emphasis on financial self-sufficiency is motivated by practical and ethical considerations; financial self-sufficiency is a necessity because it protects from sin. The Sages recognized that if a person lacks self-sufficiency, he faces many challenges to his morality, such as the temptation to steal.

Theft, however, is not the only danger. The Sages viewed this area as a slippery slope; if a person lacks financial self-sufficiency, he may eventually abandon his commitment to Torah entirely. As Rabbeinu Yonah (1200–1263) writes: "When a person does not have his own means of support, at first he will rely on gifts, but at some point these will run dry and he will resort to theft and treachery. Eventually nothing will hold him back from violating every sin in the Torah."[1] It is a classic scenario of "sin leads to sin."[2] Consequently, it is necessary for everyone, including scholars, to have a means to support themselves.

> *Self-sufficiency protects from the temptation to steal and the slippery slope of other sins.*

Since the danger is so great, it must be addressed at the earliest stages, even before a severe moral crisis materializes. When the Sages taught, "Good is Torah along with work, as toiling at both prevents sin," the sin referred to is not only stealing, rather it denotes a broad scope of sin. The combination of Torah and work prevents the sin that ultimately results from failure to support oneself, and the joint effort is indispensable in the development of a person's moral character.

Financial self-sufficiency is also valuable because it directly helps protect from infringing on the tenth commandment: the prohibition against coveting. Desiring what belongs to others is not only a great sin in and of itself, but it is also the starting point of even greater sins. The greater one's desires, the greater is the temptation to perform illicit acts to fulfill them. When a person satisfies his own needs through the labor of his hands, he has less reason to look at and desire what his neighbor has. Work and self-sufficiency are some of the strongest lines of defense against coveting.[3]

Building a Relationship with G-d

"Put not your trust in noble men, nor in a son of man." (Tehillim 146:3)

A second perspective on the importance of financial self-sufficiency focuses on the inherent value of being self-sufficient, instead of on the negative consequences of failing to maintain it. Self-sufficiency enables a person to develop spiritually because he achieves a greater trust in G-d than does a person who relies on others. If a person does not accept support from others, he can rely only on G-d to provide for him. In contrast, reliance on others detracts him from his dependence on G-d and, consequently, from his trust in G-d.

For this reason, the Sages praise a person who refuses to accept any form of charity — even if he is eligible to receive it — despite the fact that his refusal might make his life more difficult. About such a person, the prophet Yirmeyah declares, "Blessed is the man who trusts in G-d" (*Yirmeyah* 17:7). Since trust in G-d is of such great importance, it is deemed praiseworthy to maintain financial self-sufficiency even if this entails some distress.[4]

According to this understanding, "One who hates gifts shall live" because G-d provides a greater level of protection to a person who has developed a greater trust in and reliance on G-d (*Mishlei* 15:27). The ultimate expression of this trust is the rejection

> *Self-sufficiency enables man to develop his relationship with G-d since it fosters greater reliance on G-d.*

of gifts from man. One who rejects the gifts of man and depends instead on G-d's assistance becomes closer, in turn, to G-d and therefore merits life.[5]

Rabbi Samson Raphael Hirsch (1808–1888) expresses this idea as follows: "When man is independent of external things and needs, it allows for him to find his own true worth in faithfulness to G-d and his own un-disturbable happiness."[6] Man must become self-sufficient in order to develop himself and his relationship with G-d. When a person does not rely on others, he can focus on spiritual matters; it is impossible to grow spiritually when encumbered by dependencies. By developing trust in G-d through self-sufficiency, a person also strengthens all other areas of his service to G-d.

The idea that financial self-sufficiency ultimately aids a person spiritually is also articulated in a teaching of the Sages: "Greater is one who benefits from the work of his hands than a G-d-fearing person."[7]

This statement is difficult to understand. If the "one who benefits from the work of his hands" is not G-d-fearing, how can he be greater than one who is? Some suggest that both of the people in this comparison are G-d-fearing, but one lives his life with total dedication to spiritual matters, while the other spends some of his time earning a living so he can sustain himself. One might have thought that the former is greater because of his absolute dedication to G-d, but in fact, the Sages say, it is the one who benefits from the work of his hands who is greater.[8] Why is this so?

A person who fails to support himself is in danger of losing the spiritual heights he has attained because he must rely on other people. In contrast, one who works for his living must rely on G-d, thereby securing his fear of Heaven. The G-d-fearing person's dependence on others diminishes his spiritual greatness.[9]

Reliance on others diminishes a person's spiritual greatness.

Since reliance on others conjures up negative spiritual consequences, the *Chovos HaLevavos* cautions a person who desires to achieve higher levels in his service to G-d to ensure that he has a reliable means of support. Although achieving higher levels of spirituality is admirable, it entails a certain degree of *perishus*, and one's attempts to achieve spiritual greatness are inherently flawed and bound to fail if he has no means of material support. If one must rely on others, he will never achieve true *chasidus* or *perishus*. Indeed, "The foundation of *perishus* is involvement with preparing one's physical needs."[10] Just as a physical structure must be built upon a proper foundation, spiritual growth also requires that its foundation be provided for through caring for its physical needs.

The foundation of higher spiritual levels rests on a means to care for physical needs.

Living Life to Its Fullest

"Enjoy life..." (Koheles 9:9)
"A trade so that you may live...." (Kiddushin 30b)

According to a third approach, the Sages preached the value of financial self-sufficiency because it reflects the nature of the world. Self-sufficiency is to be valued in and of itself because living creatures are created with the ability to be self-sufficient. While all living things interact with the world around them in order to sustain themselves, their basic physical structure enables them to carry this out on their own. When an organism cannot operate in a self-sufficient manner, it is lacking something; it is incomplete. It follows that a person who is in need of others is not a "complete" person. Something is missing from his life.

> *Self-sufficiency is to be valued in and of itself.*

For this reason, the Sages compare a poor person to a dead person.[11] According to Rabbi Yehudah Loew, also known as the Maharal (1520–1609), the meaning of this statement is that a person who is not self-supporting does not meet the definition of a living entity by the very fact that he is not self-sustaining. In this sense, it is as if he were not alive; he is missing part of his life source. Thus, Shlomo Hamelech says, "One who hates gifts shall live" (*Mishlei* 15:27), implying that one who relies on gifts isn't living.

According to this view, self-sufficiency is not only valuable because it enables avoidance of moral challenges and because it fosters trust in G-d, but also because it is part of the very definition of life. By teaching the importance of self-sufficiency, the Sages are guiding man to live a vibrant and complete life.[12]

Along the same lines, the Sages interpret the injunction to "enjoy life" as an imperative to find a means of earning

> *Self-sufficiency is part of the definition of life.*

a living in order to support one's family or the study of Torah.[13] The word "life" metaphorically refers to livelihood, the ability to provide for oneself. Financial self-sufficiency is life-giving.[14]

The Symbol of the Olive Branch

"The dove came back to him in the evening,
and behold an olive leaf..." (Bereishis 8:11)

After the Great Flood, Noach sent a dove out from the ark to determine if the water had diminished. When it returned to the ark, the dove bore an olive branch in its beak, indicating that life had returned to the world. The olive branch is thus traditionally used to symbolize peace and the resolution of conflict.

According to the Sages, however, the olive branch has a different significance: The dove was teaching, "It is better to live from the hand of the Holy One, even if the food is bitter, than to live from the sweet things that come from man."[15]

The dove was willing to suffice with bitter olives from the hand of G-d instead of all the delights in the world provided for him by Noah. If an unintelligent bird felt this way, then certainly intelligent humans should trust in G-d to provide for their needs. And if a bird, who was not created in the image of G-d, was so loathe to accept gifts from others, then all the more should people be embarrassed to rely on others![16]

Better bitter from G-d than pleasant from people.

Refusing to take "sweet things" from man demonstrates trust in G-d and avoids the humiliation of dependence on others. The dove and its olive branch teach that it is better to do with less — and even with the bitter — than to rely on others for support.[17] As Rabbi Samson Raphael Hirsch explains, when eaten in freedom and independence, bitter and even intolerable food is sweeter than the sweetest food eaten in a dependent condition.[18]

Thus, the olive branch is a symbol of independence, freedom, and moderation. From the earliest point in history, one can learn the importance of freedom from dependence on anyone other than G-d.

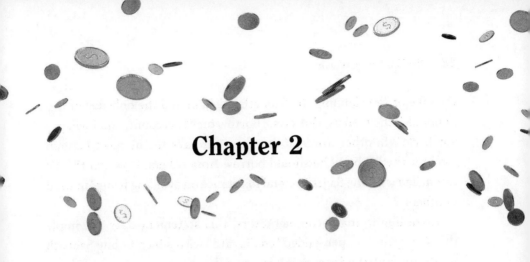

Chapter 2

Overriding Other Values

The Sages felt that the value of financial self-sufficiency is so fundamental that under certain circumstances, it can override other important and central values, such as giving up a third meal on the Sabbath and parting with personal possessions. The following sections elaborate more on these principles.

The Sabbath

"Make your Sabbath like a weekday and do not be in need of others." (Shabbos 118a)

The Sages teach that it is sometimes better to forfeit the mitzvah of eating a third meal on the Sabbath rather than accept money or food from others in order to fulfill this mitzvah.[1] Thus, if a person is financially self-sufficient, but the expense of the third meal would require that he take assistance from others, it is better to forgo this meal. Only when a person is already accepting support from others may he accept assistance for the third meal as well. Financial self-sufficiency should not be sacrificed for the sake of the third Sabbath meal.

> *Financial self-sufficiency overrides the obligation to eat the third Sabbath meal.*

Another statement of the Sages seems to contradict this ruling. For the sake of "proclaiming the Sabbath a delight and the holy day of G-d honored,"[2] they tell us, G-d says, "Borrow on My account, and I will pay you back."[3] In other words, if one does not have the money to obtain food for the Sabbath, he should borrow from others. How can this be reconciled with the Sages' general insistence on avoiding being "in need of others"?

According to many commentators, this statement does not imply that G-d gives an open-ended "credit card" with which to buy Sabbath needs. Instead, the Sages are suggesting that if a person presently lacks the necessary funds, but has good reason to anticipate that he will have the money to repay the loan in the future, he should borrow from others in order to honor the Sabbath.

A person must assess his situation to evaluate when it is appropriate to borrow for the Sabbath meals.

Thus, if a person's business is cyclical and business is slow at present, or if he knows that he has a deal in the works, he may borrow as a means of tiding himself over until he is able to once again support himself. Such a person has reason to trust that G-d will provide for him. In contrast, one who has no reasonable expectation that he will be able to repay the loan has no right to take it in order to honor the Sabbath.[4]

Interestingly, even the permission to borrow from others if one can repay the loan in the future is limited to the case of the Sabbath. Only in this case does G-d promise, "Borrow on My account and I will pay you back." There is no dispensation to

Most personal possessions should be sold if necessary to maintain self-sufficiency.

borrow money in order to enable the performance of other mitzvos.

Personal Possessions

"Sell before you come to poverty…" (*Yevamos 63a*)

The Sages placed such great importance on the value of self-sufficiency that they insisted one be prepared to sell his personal possessions rather than fall into poverty. Businesses do not always succeed and investments sometimes go sour, but even when one's attempts at building a livelihood fail, he should do his utmost to maintain his self-sufficiency. Although certain personal items, such as clothing, should not be sold even in dire circumstances, a person must be willing to part with his other belongings in order to maintain himself. Financial self-sufficiency is deemed more important than material possessions.[5]

Personal Honor

"Better off is the lowly one who serves for his keep than the pompous one who lacks bread." (Mishlei 12:9)

The Torah grants great significance to an individual's personal honor and dignity. A person must possess the appropriate measure of self-esteem — recognition of his own self-worth — so that he will not act in a degrading manner. But even personal dignity has its limits. While it is appropriate to take precautions to protect one's honor, there are values that supersede its importance.

Thus, the Sages teach, "A person should always hire himself out to work that is strange to him rather than be in need of others."[6] If a person's circumstances create a situation in which he must choose between his own honor and a means of livelihood, he should forgo his honor and take the job, even if it is menial or beneath his dignity. It is certainly preferable to salvage one's financial situation while maintaining honor if possible. Nonetheless, if no other option is available, one must choose any means of supporting himself: He must go to work.[7]

People should never become so haughty that they prefer to be supported by others rather than work. Indeed, Rabbi Moshe Chaim Luzzatto (1707–1746) writes that only the most foolish people would prefer to be supported by others rather than to be self-supporting.[8]

The concept of maintaining self-sufficiency is so important that it not only overrides personal honor, but even the honor of the Torah. Certain activities are deemed inappropriate for a Torah scholar because he represents the honor of the Torah, and these acts may degrade that honor. Thus, the scholar should dress in a manner that brings honor to the Torah and avoid doing anything in public that could possibly disgrace the honor of Heaven.[9] If, however, the Torah scholar must engage in a menial activity in order to support himself, it is permitted for him to do so, notwithstanding the honor of the Torah. No matter what the job entails, it does not bring dishonor to the Torah because the scholar performs the task in order to support himself. Based on this, the Talmud says it is better for a scholar to skin hides of slaughtered animals in public to earn a living, rather than say about himself that he is a distinguished person and such work is beneath his dignity. Under other circumstances this work would have been inappropriate for him to do, but since he engages in this activity to earn a livelihood it is permissible and does not disgrace the honor of the Torah.[10]

Living in the Land of Israel

"It is better to live outside the Land if one has the ability to support himself there than it is to live in the Land if one will need to be supported by the community."
(Chochmas Adam)

In many contexts, the Sages stressed the importance of living in the Land of Israel, going so far as to say that "if one lives outside of the Land of Israel, it is like he serves idolatry," and "it is better to live in the Land of Israel in a city whose majority are idolaters, rather than live outside the Land of Israel in a city whose majority is Jewish."[11] Nevertheless, in *Chochmas Adam*, Rabbi Avraham Danzig (1748–1820) writes that one should not move to the Land of Israel if that will entail relying on others for support. The importance of self-sufficiency outweighs even the great advantages of living in the Holy Land![12]

> *Self-sufficiency overrides the significance of living in the land of Israel.*

More Rather Than Less

"There is an evil I have observed beneath the sun." (Koheles 6:1)

One of the evils of this world, as mentioned in *Koheles*, is that a person can acquire wealth yet he is unable to enjoy it when he passes on to the next world. Those that remain after him, some of whom may even be his enemies, will take pleasure in it. Despite this possibility, one of the early Jewish writers states that it is better to leave over wealth even if one's enemies will benefit from it rather than be in need of one's friend while still alive.[13] Thus, in providing for one's needs, a person need not cut things down to the bone, as one never knows what his needs will be.

One example of this is when preparing for retirement. A person doesn't know how long he will live so he must take steps to provide for himself in case he lives to a ripe old age. People shouldn't tell themselves that because they are old and can't take their wealth with them to the next world that they need not engage in economic activity. No one wants to come up short in later years,

> *It is better to leave over wealth even if others will benefit from it than to be in need of others while still alive.*

so it is better to have too much than not enough. The underlying concept is that is better not to be in need of others, even if wealth is left over.

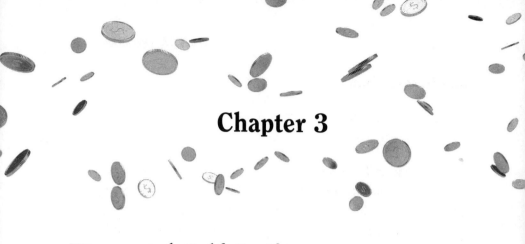

Chapter 3

Financial Self-Sufficiency and Mitzvos

The importance of financial self-sufficiency is emphasized in the fulfillment of a number of mitzvos in the Torah, such as saying grace after a meal, offering first fruits, and more. The following sections will explore these and other mitzvos and how they relate to financial self-sufficiency.

Grace after Meals

"And you will eat and be satisfied and you will bless the Lord your G-d." (Devarim 8:10)

In the Grace After Meals,[1] one recognizes G-d's role in providing for daily needs. After beseeching Him for continued support with the words, "tend us, nourish us, sustain us," the prayer concludes with a request that reflects appreciation of the importance of financial self-sufficiency: "Please, make us not needful of the gifts of human hands, nor of their loans, but only of Your hand, which is full, open, holy, and generous." By including this request in the text of an oft-recited blessing, the Sages wished to impart this message to the entire nation. Every time a person benefits from G-d's bounty, he reminds himself that it is best to rely solely on His generosity. Essentially, the request is that G-d help man trust in — and depend on — Him alone by removing the obstacle that is obstructing him from doing so: trust in, and dependence on, other people.[2] If taken at face value, the blessing teaches one not to be in need of other people, but if a person relies on himself — his ingenuity, his strength or his own wealth — then it is okay. In truth this is incorrect. At its

> *The Grace after Meals teaches that G-d is the true source of sustenance.*

highest level, the concept of trust in G-d excludes trust in anything other than in G-d, including trust in oneself. The *Chovos HaLevavos*, in his introduction to his treatise on trust in G-d, states that trust is the single most important quality for a person who is a servant of G-d; it is indispensable.[3] At its core, this quality calls man to recognize G-d's role in every aspect of life and to conduct his life accordingly. Consequently, the *Chovos HaLevavos* writes that even trust in one's own wisdom, power, or wealth reflects a lack of trust in G-d. Similarly, trust or reliance on a job, employer, or business also detracts from — and even contradicts — trust in G-d. The Grace after Meals is focused on what is perhaps the most common challenge to reliance on G-d, namely taking from other people. Still it alludes to the larger concept of not relying on anything other than G-d as it concludes, "but only of Your Hand."

First Fruits

"My father was a poor Aramean." (*Devarim* 26:5)

According to many commentators, the Aramean referred to in the verse above is Yaakov, who lived with his father-in-law, Lavan, in Aram. The Torah uses the Hebrew word — *oved* — in reference to Yaakov, which literally means "lost." The word can also be understood to mean "poor," as in the verse, "Give drink to the *oved*" (*Mishlei* 31:6).[4] What is it that poverty and being lost have in common that makes it possible for one word to reflect both meanings?

A life of poverty often lacks stability and requires a person to wander in search of sustenance. This is part of being lost in this world. A man lacks standing, a firm base of support.[5] In contrast, financial self-sufficiency enables a person to find his way and to achieve his unique potential. It helps protect from becoming lost in this world.[6]

Interestingly, the section of *"Arami oved avi"* (my father was a poor Aramean) is recited along with the offering of the First Fruits in the Temple.[7] The farmer who brings his First Fruits to Jerusalem is a land-owner; he has ample food and is part of a thriving, independent nation. At that juncture, he must recognize G-d's role in his success, and he highlights G-d's benevolence by comparing his situation to that of his forefather, Yaakov. When Yaakov set out for Aram, he was completely impoverished, and was thus essentially "lost." He lacked nearly everything and was entirely reliant on the goodwill of Lavan. When we come to recite this text in conjunction with bringing the First Fruits to the Temple we recognize that with G-d's help, we have come so far — from homelessness, poverty, and dependence — to a bountiful land and a state of self-sufficiency. One who brings the First Fruits gives thanks for the great transformation that has taken place, the transformation from *oved* to financial self-sufficiency.

> *One who brings the First Fruits gives thanks for his financial self-sufficiency.*

Yours Come First

"His lost object and that of his fathers, his own comes first." (Bava Metzia 33a)

It is clear from many laws relating to money that a general principle operates when conflict arises between one's own monetary interests and that of others.[8] The rule is that a person has the right to take care of his own first: A person need not experience financial loss in order to help somebody else avoid a loss.

> *The general principle is that when a conflict arises, personal financial interests come before those of other people.*

Thus, while many mitzvos require a person to be concerned with the property and belongings of others, it becomes obligatory only if this concern is not in conflict with personal financial interests.

For example, the commandment to return lost property to others is predicated on the concern for other people's property. However, what happens if returning the lost object will force the finder to take time off from work, which in turn will be detrimental to his own income? In such a case, he is not obligated to return the item unless the owner is going to pay him.[9] The returning of an item free of charge is only when a person is unemployed and the activity involves no personal loss. The reason for this is that one's own financial interests take priority. While it is important to maintain value and property for others, there is no obligation to sustain monetary loss in order to do so.

In the area of social duties, the Torah recognizes the importance of an individual's existence and independence. Indeed, this recognition is at the foundation of numerous monetary laws. Self-concern comes before self-forgetting sacrifice. The establishment of society requires that this be the normal principle of social life, as it could not function if it were to insist on an over-abundance of kindness.[10]

Despite the principle that a person has the right to put his own monetary concerns before those of other people, the Sages cautioned against its abuse. A delicate balance must be maintained. While a person must care for his own financial well-being, he should not misuse this rule to justify the abandonment of charitable acts and generosity. It is always possible to find some sort of personal need to prioritize before the needs of others. The Sages therefore recommend that one go beyond the letter of the law and help others unless a significant personal loss will result. Indeed, they stress that failure to follow this approach may lead to personal financial disaster; one who avoids helping others will eventually find himself in need — *middah k'neged middah* (measure for measure).[11]

> *The establishment of a functioning society requires that self-concern come prior to self-sacrifice.*

So while the strict law could perhaps enable a person to justify a life of self-interest, this is not the way a person should live his life.[12] What is necessary is a balanced perspective. Self-sufficiency should not be used as an excuse to ignore the needs of others.

> *A balanced perspective between taking cares of one's own financial needs and those of others is necessary.*

Gifts

"One who hates gifts will live." (*Mishlei* 15:27)

As previously seen, one of the ramifications of maintaining financial self-sufficiency is distancing oneself from receiving gifts of monetary support.[13] Maimonides, known as Rambam (1135–1204), states that the truly righteous refuse to take gifts from others, preferring to put their trust entirely in G-d.[14]

"One who hates gifts will live" is an explicit reference to the importance of maintaining financial self-sufficiency. One who avoids reliance on others will ultimately "live" and succeed. The negative attitude toward gifts grows out of two considerations:

- Firstly, any time a person receives a gift from another person it creates a conflict with trust in G-d. There is always the risk that the recipient will see the role others play in his life and fail to see G-d's part. Consequently, the way of the very righteous was always to reject gifts from others.[15]
- Secondly, the Sages had a negative view of gifts since they placed a premium on being satisfied with that which is necessary and they avoided seeking luxuries. In their view, the pursuit of these extras stems from a misplaced love of this world, growing out of jealousy, desire, and longing for honor. These qualities are

> *The rejection of gifts reflects an emphasis in trusting G-d as well as an emphasis on needs over wants.*

all detrimental to a person's spiritual well-being and in their words, "they take the person out of this world" (*Avos* 4:21). In contrast, satisfaction with what is necessary in this world is a path toward success both in this world and the next. Gifts reflect a need for more than is necessary, and thus the very righteous are not interested in assistance from people.[16]

While "hating gifts" seems like a philosophical theory, it actually has legal ramifications as well. The Talmud discusses a case in which an inherited property is to be divided between two brothers. Can the wealthy brother suggest that his poorer brother receive a larger portion? Even though this seems like a generous offer in his favor, the Talmud states that the poorer brother cannot be forced to accept this division of property. If his brother tells him to pay for the additional portion, he can claim that he does not have the money to buy it, and if his brother wishes to give him the extra portion as a gift, he can insist that he is not interested in gifts — for "one who hates gifts will live." Every individual has a right to financial self-sufficiency; no one can be compelled to accept a gift.

Hospitality

"One who wishes to benefit [from others]
should benefit like Elisha." (*Berachos* 10b)

Although the acceptance of gifts is strongly discouraged, gifts are not always a threat to self-sufficiency. When they are received in the appropriate context and with the appropriate intentions, the Sages attested to their acceptability.

The book of Kings recounts the hospitality of the Shunamit woman, who provided lodging and basic amenities to the prophet Elisha (*Melachim II* 4). The Sages teach that one should benefit from others only in the manner that Elisha benefited from the Shunamit woman. What does this mean? How can one reconcile this statement, which assumes it is sometimes permissible to rely on others, with the Sages' general guidance not to take from others?

One approach suggests that Elisha did not accept gifts or money from others; rather, he accepted their hospitality. This type of generosity can be accepted without violating the principle of "not needing others."[17] Hospitality is not a gift or support; it is a manner of receiving guests.

Others suggest that it is acceptable to accept a gift if in so doing the recipient also benefits the giver. By accepting their hospitality, Elisha was honoring the Shunamite woman and her husband and allowing them the opportunity to have a relationship with a great prophet. Under such circumstances, it is not only permissible — but also desirable — to accept something from the other person. The recipient, in a sense, becomes the giver.[18]

Indeed, it was a common practice among the prophets to accept small gifts from worthy people.[19] Interestingly, accepting such gifts was limited to people who could benefit from the relationship. These gifts were viewed by the prophets as gifts from G-d, and only if they came from "good people" could it take on this status. In addition, by accepting the gift the giver would actually receive a benefit, as the gift fostered a connection with the prophet similar to his accepting hospitality discussed above. This connection could only be fostered when the giver had the appropriate intent such as to honor the prophet. The Talmud even compares such gifts to bringing First Fruits to the Temple. This correlation only has meaning if the giver has a proper intent.[20] By contrast, when Rabbeinu Yonah discusses the problems of not having a means of self-sufficiency, he says that a person will come to seek and take gifts by flattering even the wicked.[21] Gifts from the wicked could never be viewed as "gifts from G-d."

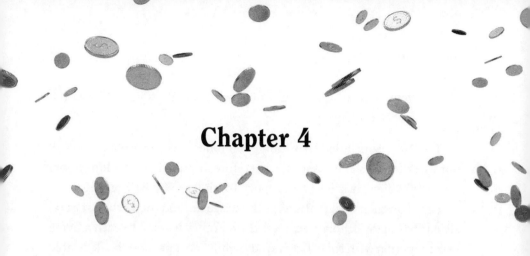

Chapter 4

Torah Study and Self-Sufficiency

"Accustom them to derech eretz [a livelihood]
along with their Torah." (*Berachos 35b*)

As has already been seen, the Torah and Sages reiterate the importance of working to make a living and avoidance of dependence on others to the extent that this value overrides many other important values.
At the same time, Torah study is one of the highest values in the life of a
Jew. Clearly, a conflict can arise between the demands of intense Torah
study and the need to earn a living. How does intense study of Torah
that occupies one's day and night co-exist with working the land and
laboring for one's livelihood? This is an ancient problem that has been
addressed in the Talmud.

The Talmud records a debate between Rabbi Shimon Bar Yochai and
Rabbi Yishmael regarding the proper resolution of this dilemma. On one
hand, the Torah states, "You may gather in your grain, your wine, and
your oil" (*Devarim* 11:14). On the other hand, there is a command to
study Torah day and night (*Yehoshua* 1:8). Two solutions were offered:

- Rabbi Shimon Bar Yochai was of the opinion that one should
  dedicate himself exclusively to Torah, and his work will then be
  taken care of by others.
- Rabbi Yishmael maintained, however, "*hanheg bahem minhag*

derech eretz," that one should work in addition to dedicating himself to Torah.

The Sages concluded that Rabbi Shimon Bar Yochai's approach will not work for everyone, and it is therefore appropriate to adopt Rabbi Yishmael's view; it is best to support Torah learning by working.

Based on their observations of the world around them, the Sages realized that many scholars succeeded when they worked to earn a living in conjunction with their Torah study, while most people who dedicated themselves entirely to Torah ultimately failed.[1]

Why is this so? Rashi (1040–1105) suggests that if a scholar does not support himself, he will need to rely on others, and this will lead to *bitul Torah* (the forsaking of his studies).[2] A scholar might think he is avoiding wasting his precious time by dedicating himself solely to his studies, but ultimately, dependency actually produces the opposite effect. When one is unsure of how he will take care of his needs, his situation is precarious and his Torah studies suffer. It is better to work a certain number of hours and have the stability to focus on one's learning than to endure the never-ending stress of not knowing from where the next meal will come. Ultimately, this situation can deteriorate to the point where he is forced to give up Torah entirely or resort to undesirable approaches to sustain himself.

Similarly, Shlomo Hamelech teaches, "Good is inheritance with wisdom" (*Koheles* 7:11), and the Sages insist, "If there is no flour, there is no Torah."[3] When one's physical needs are not properly met — when there is no "flour" — it is difficult to study properly, either because one must take the time to find alternative means of support or because he will be distracted by his financial concerns.[4] When one's basic needs are provided for, his Torah is also secure.[5]

Rabbeinu Yonah suggests an additional reason as to why it is important for a scholar to support himself. If the needs of scholars are placed on the shoulders of others, the scholar's status will be lowered in the eyes of the public, and he will therefore have less influence in guiding the people — "a poor man's wisdom is despised and his words go unheeded" (*Koheles* 9:16). Lack of self-sufficiency negates one of the crucial roles of the scholar.[6]

Others offer still another reason as to why it is of great value for a scholar to support himself. They explain that if a scholar relies on others for monetary support, he will lose the merit that accrues through his pursuit of wisdom and service of G-d. He becomes the source of great merit for others, but not for himself. If he wishes to reap the full benefit of his scholarship and piety, then the scholar must support himself.[7] This concept is encapsulated in the *Chovos HaLevavos*: "The foundation of *perishus* [separation from worldly matters] is involvement with preparing one's physical needs."[8]

In summary, there are at least three reasons why it is preferable for a scholar to have a means of self-support:

- Self-sufficiency makes his scholarship secure and frees his mind from financial worries.
- It helps maintain his stature in the eyes of the people and allows him to have more influence.
- Self-sufficiency enables the scholar to retain the merit that he has earned from G-d for his efforts.

Consequently, the Torah's statement, "You may gather in your grain, your wine, and your oil," represents the preservation of the Torah, not its antithesis.

While it certainly is preferable for the scholar to have financial self-sufficiency,[9] many of the later commentators write that what was true in earlier times is not always feasible in later generations. Thus, in modern times when it is difficult to excel in Torah scholarship and support oneself at the same time, if necessary, it is preferable for the scholar to receive support.[10] This is particularly true in his formative years.

Primacy of Torah Learning

"Make your Torah learning a fixed practice." (Avos 1:15)

Although the Sages concluded that it is best to work to support oneself and one's Torah learning, they repeatedly stressed that one's primary concern should be his studies, not his involvement in self-support.[11]

> *Though self-sufficiency is important, the purpose of our physical work is to support our spiritual pursuits.*

Thus, although a scholar must be involved in *derech eretz* (an occupation), his Torah studies should be "fixed," a scheduled commitment, so that they are regular part of his daily routine. The purpose of his mundane endeavors is to support his spiritual pursuits.

Torah study is "fixed" on a quantitative and qualitative level. One must set aside a certain amount of time to devote to Torah. Minimally, a person is required to set time aside for study during the day and night; ideally, he should spend the better part of his day immersed in the study of Torah. Indeed, while difficult today, Rambam describes the ideal day of a Jew as including nine hours of study and three hours of work![12] The fixed nature of Torah study also reflects that it, not his livelihood, is the

> *The fixed nature of Torah study also reflects that it is the primary and central goal of a Jew's life.*

primary and central goal of a Jew's life. No matter how much time he ultimately devotes to study, one's approach to learning should not be haphazard; he should not learn only when he finds the time. Rather, his daily schedule should be focused around his learning. All of his activities to support himself should revolve around this goal.[13]

This concept is alluded to by the Sages when they contrasted fixed Torah study with work that should be subsidiary to it (*Berachos* 35b). His work must revolve around Torah; Torah study should not revolve around his work or other activities. Conceptually and practically, Torah should be the focal point of one's life.[14]

This Mishnaic concept agrees with the thrust of the Sages' statement, "If there is no Torah, there is no flour."[15] While financial self-sufficiency is critical for success in Torah learning, at the same time, one's material success depends on his Torah. There are two aspects to man: the physical and spiritual, the body and soul. Ultimately what makes man unique among the creation is his soul. The body is the home for the soul — and of course must be taken care of — but man's purpose is to nurture and help his soul flourish. One way in which this is done is by uplifting physical acts and giving them spiritual meaning. One of the prime purposes of earning a living is to enable one to engage in Torah study and other mitzvah-like endeavors. Wealth that doesn't support spiritual activities is viewed by the Sages as hollow. As a result, if a person possesses no Torah, his wealth

Wealth without Torah is empty, leaving the wealth without significance.

fails to achieve its purpose and lacks meaning entirely.[16]

Effort in Torah

"One who fulfills the Torah when he is poor will eventually fulfill it with wealth." (Avos 4:11)

The Divine scheme of reward and punishment is *middah k'neged middah*; they relate directly to the good deed or transgression. This provides man the opportunity to recognize what he has done wrong and return to G-d. Thus, the Mishnah teaches, if man sets time aside to study Torah on a regular basis, even though he is involved with the pursuit of a livelihood, in the end he will merit the ability to study Torah without the burdens of livelihood. The learning of Torah under challenging conditions can create future opportunities under more pleasant circumstances. Similarly, if a wealthy person fails to learn Torah because his

A relationship exists between the effort and energy a person puts into the study of Torah and that which he puts into monetary pursuits.

wealth prevents him from learning, in the end he will not have the opportunity to learn because of poverty.[17]

A relationship exists between the effort and energy a person puts into the study of Torah and that which he puts into monetary pursuits. A person can choose where to put his efforts, but he must be conscious that there are consequences for his decisions.

Staying Focused

"Praiseworthy is the person who listens to me, to hasten to my doors every day, to the doorposts of my entranceways." (Mishlei 8:34)

Rambam writes that there are different levels of fulfillment of the mitzvah of *talmud Torah* (Torah study). The lowest level is to learn in order to satisfy the basic requirement of daily study. On a higher level, one pursues Torah learning not only to fulfill the requirement, but also out of a quest to understand G-d's word. A person who chooses to study Torah on this level can ultimately merit "the crown of Torah," reflecting his dedication to focused Torah study. Rambam notes that although such a person has a single-minded focus on Torah, and "he should not remove his mind to other things," he must nonetheless have a means of support, which may include some sort of livelihood.[18] This is not contradictory. While this person spends most of his time in study and his mind is occupied with Torah, he also takes time to maintain his physical existence — including pursuit of a livelihood — without detracting from his primary goal.

> One challenge the Torah scholar faces is maintaining his dedication despite his involvement in self-support.

The Talmud relates that Shmuel, one of the great Sages of the Talmud, commented that he was not as great as his father, for his father would check into his business and other involvements twice a day, while he did so only once. Why does the fact that Shmuel's father would leave his Torah studies *more* than Shmuel reflect greatness? Shmuel was commenting on his father's ability to inspect his business and property and to then shift back into the study of Torah. He was able to maintain his focus on Torah despite having to check his business twice a day.[19]

The Right Time

"Is this a [proper] time to accept money [with which],
to buy clothing, olive trees, vineyards, sheep, cattle,
slaves, and maidservants?" (Melachim II 5:26)

In the verse above, the prophet Elisha was speaking to his servant Gehazi. His message was that it is inappropriate for the members of the prophet's school to partake in activities that are acceptable for most people.[20] In more contemporary terminology, his point was that while the yeshiva is in session, it is incumbent on teachers and students to dedicate themselves wholeheartedly to the mission and purpose of the yeshiva: Torah learning.

Often in life, what is appropriate on one occasion maybe inappropriate on another. One of the most famous teachings from the book of *Koheles* is that everything in this world has an appropriate time, "A time to plant and a time to uproot..." (*Koheles* 3:2). This includes seeking a livelihood. Once a person has a wife and home, he has many monetary obligations and of necessity he must find a livelihood.[21] In contrast, for a student in yeshiva during his formative years, it may be inappropriate to pursue a livelihood.[22] When one is enrolled in yeshiva, his Torah study demands complete dedication to the goals and purposes of the yeshiva; this is not the time for accumulating monetary wealth.

The early years of a Torah scholar's studies are the foundation of a lifetime of learning, and a foundation must be built differently than the rest of the structure in order to provide support. Thus, the Sages emphasized the necessity for the student to limit his physical needs so that he can excel in Torah: "This is the way of Torah, bread with salt you shall eat and measured water you will drink."[23] In particular, this applies to the early years of study. These are

> *Everything has an appropriate time. The early period in a scholar's development will be different from the later periods with respect to his involvement in money matters.*

seminal years, a time to focus entirely on personal growth through Torah; a time to be satisfied with a little so that one can excel in his learning.[24]

Link in the Tradition

"Moshe received the Torah at Sinai and gave it to Yehoshua, and Yehoshua to the Elders, and the Elders to the Prophets, and the Prophets to the men of the Great Assembly." (Avos 1:1)

Without question, working hard to earn a living can impede the serious study of Torah. It can drain a person's physical and mental energy to the point where he is exhausted and left without the wherewithal for study. Nonetheless, the obligation to study remains even in the face of these challenges.

Some of the greatest Sages worked at jobs that were physically draining. Abba Hilkiah worked digging the earth, Hillel chopped wood, Rabbi Yehoshua was a smith, and Rav Huna was a water carrier.[25] Despite limitations on their time and energy, they continued to learn and became great Torah scholars. Many ultimately became the primary links in the great chain of tradition that links the transmission of Torah from Moshe down through the ages to the scholars of each generation.[26]

> *Earning a livelihood did not discourage or prevent some of the greatest scholars from excelling in their studies.*

The Source of True Happiness

"I rejoiced over your word like one who finds abundant spoils." (Tehillim 119:162)

Scripture often uses wealth as a metaphor for Torah and wisdom. Just as increasing one's wealth brings great joy, learning and understanding

Torah should also bring happiness.[27] Torah should not be viewed as a yoke or burden, but rather as a source of pleasure.

Indeed, the pleasure of Torah has no earthly comparison, but the joy of obtaining wealth can be used to describe it to some degree. Thus, Scripture repeats that Torah is more valuable than any amount of wealth, "The Torah of Your mouth is better for me than thousands in gold and silver" (*Tehillim* 119:72). Similarly, "Accept my discipline, and not silver; knowledge is choicer than fine gold. For wisdom is greater than pearls; no possessions can be compared to it" (*Mishlei* 8:10–11). The verse teaches that it is more worthwhile to put energy into Torah than into acquiring ephemeral wealth. Effort

> *Ultimately, financial self-sufficiency has the goal of supporting greater spirituality.*

must be made to acquire wisdom, to achieve it with energy and zeal, rather than to put time and efforts into achieving material success.

In this realm, like many others, the Jew is enjoined to be a contrarian, to choose a path that differs from those around him. While the Torah path encourages self-sufficiency, that same financial self-sufficiency itself has only one goal: greater spirituality. The key to remaining on the Torah path is to appreciate that "no possessions can be compared to it!"[28]

So the Torah Should Not Be Forgotten

"For it is a time to act for G-d." (*Tehillim* 119:126)

Although a discussion of the contemporary *kollel* is beyond the scope of this work, it is necessary to say a few words on the topic, since there are aspects of the *kollel* that would appear inconsistent with concepts emphasized by the Sages as discussed in earlier sections.

As in many areas of life, there are often conflicts between two or more important values. This is the case when it comes to the *kollel*. While the *kollel* reflects the importance of Torah study, it may at the same time run counter to traditional values of financial self-sufficiency. This section will focus on the basic concepts relevant to this topic as seen from sources, but will not look at the details of any contemporary situation. Understanding the issues surrounding the *kollel* paradigm requires a look at the halachic issues that arise from it.

The primary concept that must be understood is the permissibility to receive money for Torah. During the Middle Ages, a major dispute arose about whether rabbis may receive compensation. Rambam and others wrote, in very strong words, that this was not only prohibited but was a desecration of G-d's name. The opposing position, articulated at length by the Rabbi Shimon ben Tzemach Duran (also known as the Tashbetz, 1361–1444), argued not only was it permissible but that the community is obligated to support him. Rabbi Yosef Karo, after suggesting how the proofs of Rambam can be refuted, commented that often when there is a doubt in how the law should be concluded, the approach should be to observe the common practice at the time.[29] On this he noted that the common practice before and after the time of Rambam was that rabbis received money from the community. Indeed, this has continued to be the common practice until today. These sources allowed rabbis to receive communal money because they were providing a service to the community. They were paid to be in a position of leadership. In addition, this position stipulated that in order to be eligible the scholar needed to be on a high level and worthy of a leadership position. This conclusion and practice would not allow for members of a *kollel* to take money since in most instances the typical member of a *kollel* would not qualify under these guidelines.[30]

Rabbi Karo also cites another reason why the practice is not in accordance with Rambam and those that supported his position. He says the situation is like an emergency where the rule of "It is a time to act for G-d" should be invoked. This rule is a special dispensation that allows for certain rules to be relaxed in order to preserve the Torah. Rabbi Karo argued that if the Rabbis do not receive a salary, they will not be able to study properly and the Torah itself will be forgotten; hence the necessitation that communities support their rabbis.

This allowance, based on "it is a time to act for G-d," can also be invoked to support a *kollel*. The *kollel* can be viewed as an extension of this dispensation if the continuity of Torah is seen as endangered.[31]

Although the *kollel* can be viewed in the context of "it is a time to act for G-d," it clearly is a new application of the emergency concept, and there are differences between the *kollel* and traditional support of rabbis. These differences are both in terms of the permission to take money and also in the consequences of its implementation.

While there are a number of differences between the *kollel* and traditional support of the Rabbi, here the focus will be limited to the topic at hand.

The *kollel* extends this concept to include people who do not serve the community in an overt way. Certainly, a community can pay people for their services; but this usually means they provide a specific service. Traditionally, Torah study was not viewed as a service for which monetary compensation was granted. Thus, earlier sources never applied the emergency clause to people learning Torah, in distinction to a person who serves in the positon of a judge, who is providing a necessary service, and is paid to fill that position.[32]

Another aspect of its broadening the concept of paying people to be engaged in the study of Torah was that the *kollel* was for married men who had an obligation to support themselves and their wives. The common practice in the past was to support rabbis who served the community in a formal capacity, and perhaps some unmarried students of the Rabbi. In those days, at least, this was sufficient to preserve the Torah. This expansion creates a conflict with the concept of scholars — and certainly students — supporting themselves.

Despite these distinctions, and others that are beyond the scope of this book, it can be suggested that whatever changes and fallout develop from the *kollel*, it is all included in the fundamental dispensation of "for it is a time to act for G-d."[33] This overrides other considerations in order to preserve the Torah.

As mentioned in the introduction to this book, conflicts between different values often arise and it is necessary to seek guidance on how to resolve the tension between them. This is such a situation. Each person has his own unique set of circumstances and needs to find the approach that is appropriate for him. As such, he should seek rabbinic guidance from a rabbi who knows him.[34]

Part II

Establishing and Maintaining
Financial Self-Sufficiency

Financial self-sufficiency is not just a concept or theory; it is a path that requires implementation, and implementation is no small task. Establishing and maintaining financial self-sufficiency includes many different elements. The most basic components are to generate a source of income and to ensure that expenses don't surpass income. Beyond this it is usually necessary to invest and to take steps to protect assets. In other words, it takes planning and foresight to maintain the self-sufficiency a person hopes to create through work or business.

This section will look at the guidance the Sages provide in finding a source of income and choosing a career. It will also examine some of the Sages' teachings and perspectives toward work in general.

As mentioned, no matter how much income a person generates, if expenses surpass income it will be impossible to maintain financial independence. The Sages also give guidance about how to spend wealth, and provide principles and advice in the realm of financial planning. Planning is a crucial part of finances, as it helps solidify and truly maintain financial self-sufficiency over the course of time.

Finally, it is important to look at the role of trust in G-d as it relates to livelihood. The advice and guidance the Sages provide is not fundamentally economic; ultimately, it is to help us live as servants of G-d. Pursuit of livelihood can readily come into conflict with trust in G-d, so it is essential to understand how this concept relates to earning a living.

It is worth noting that the Sages were men of great wisdom. They understood that their teachings couldn't be limited to a specific time or place, even when relating to very practical issues such as work, spending, and investing. Instead of telling people what to do, they gave guiding principles. Today's world is vastly different than that of the Sages, yet their teachings are as relevant today as they were two thousand years ago.

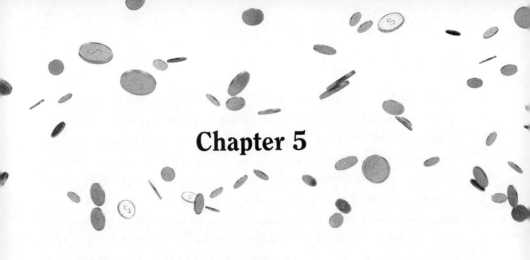

Chapter 5

Paths to Livelihood

Clearly, self-sufficiency requires a person to find a means of support. While monetary self-sufficiency is the primary purpose in seeking a livelihood, a person must consider many different factors when choosing a particular approach to supporting himself. Each person is unique and has distinct needs, desires, talents, and circumstances that affect his choice. The Sages gave broad guidance to help people find their occupation.

Education

"Just as a father must teach his son Torah,
so too he must teach him a trade." (Kiddushin 30b)

The Talmud indicates that a parent has a formal obligation to teach his child a trade or how to conduct a business; however, this obligation is not recorded by all of the later authorities as an actual obligation.[1] Nonetheless, all agree that teaching a child a trade or a business is significant and has a special status in Torah law.

> *Teaching a child a trade is a mitzvah.*

Providing a child with the ability to earn a living is significant because it is part of the necessary training for independent life that is the responsibility of every parent. This gives it a mitzvah-like quality. Thus, although the Torah prohibits conducting business on the Sabbath, it is permissible on the Sabbath to arrange for a teacher to teach one's child a trade.[2] If not for the mitzvah component, such activity would certainly be prohibited. This is similar to arranging marriages and making charitable donations on the Sabbath. While marriages are not performed on the Sabbath, arranging for them is allowed because it is a mitzvah. The same is true of charitable donations, where although the money itself can not be given, a commitment can be made. Similarly, if a father accidentally kills his son while teaching him a trade, he is not compelled to flee to one of the cities of refuge,[3] since the death occurred while in the process of performing a mitzvah.[4]

According to the Talmud, the importance of teaching others a trade by which they can support themselves was one of the ideas stressed by

> *Teaching a child a trade not only helps the child, but benefits society as a whole.*

Yisro to his son-in-law, Moshe. According to the Talmud, when Yisro told Moshe, "and you shall make known to them the path" (*Shemos* 18:20), he was alluding to the "house of their lives" which is a reference to having a trade as a means of economic self-sufficiency. When people have a means of support, there are fewer thefts, and thus the court case load is reduced.[5] Consequently, he hinted to this concept while instructing Moshe how to establish a court system, since self-sufficiency has a direct impact on the courts. Thus, aside from benefiting the individual, teaching a person a trade benefits society as a whole.

Choosing a Vocation

"Wealth and poverty are not in the profession; every profession has those who are wealthy and those who are poor." (Kiddushin 82a)

Each person is unique and has his special talents and interests. As a result, not all jobs are appropriate for all people. Each person must find the vocation that best suits his unique qualities.

This is similar to what can be observed in the animal kingdom. Each creature is unique and has its own particular way of providing for itself and surviving the tribulations of nature. Some are herbivores and others are carnivores; some swim and others fly. G-d created them with what they need to survive. Similarly, each person has a unique path in this world, including the means of support appropriate for him or her.[6]

> *Each person needs to determine the field that is most suitable for him or her based on his unique set of talents and capabilities.*

Although animals instinctively take action in accordance with their capabilities, people must discern for themselves what suits them best. Without question, making this determination can be a challenging task, but when a person finds the work most suited for his abilities and personality, he will ultimately derive more satisfaction from it.[7]

All Are Beautiful

"He made everything beautiful in its time." (Koheles 3:11)

Every society has many different tasks and functions that people must carry out in order for it to function properly. Some of the necessary jobs are not glamorous; some are even menial or distasteful. Nonetheless, all are vital. In order to ensure that people will fill all of the positions, G-d created the world in such a way that all people can see their vocations in a positive light, even if they may be unappealing to most others. Not only can they view their less-desirable jobs positively, but they don't need to view them in any other way. In their eyes, their profession is respectable and makes an important contribution to the overall good of society.

> *All occupations contribute to society and can be seen in a positive light.*

This is one way to understand the verse, "He has also put an enigma into their minds so that man cannot comprehend what G-d had done from beginning to end" (*Koheles* 3:11). In other words, G-d made man in such a way that he need not see the negative aspects of his trade.[8]

Although all types of occupations are necessary, not all are recommended. Consequently, the Sages offered general guidance regarding the choice of a profession conducive to Torah learning and avoidance of sin. While they recommended that people avoid certain trades and professions, they were confident that some people would not follow their sage advice, and that the other jobs necessary for a functioning society would thus be filled as well.[9]

Following in Parents' Footsteps

"Do not change from the profession of your fathers!" (Arachin 16b)

Although each person has his own unique talents, skills, and interests, choosing the same business as one's parents offers some advantages. One of the most obvious is a situation in which a parent has built a business. If this business has a satisfied clientele and a good reputation, then the child is already ahead of the game; he enters into a business that is developed and profitable, thus avoiding many of the challenges otherwise faced in the world of business.[10]

> *When possible, a child should give serious consideration to following in the footsteps of his parents.*

Moreover, in such a situation, the child already knows the business or trade. He is accustomed to it and knows its benefits along with its downsides. Since he comes into the trade already familiar with and accustomed to the more negative aspects of the industry, they may not bother him, and he will thus have more positive feelings about his livelihood.[11]

Contributing to Society

"[They are disqualified from testifying as witnesses
and serving as Judges] because they do not involve
themselves in contributing to society..." (Sanhedrin 24b)

One piece of guidance the Sages provided regarding choice of vocation is that a person should aim to contribute to society in some capacity. The Sages frowned upon those whose occupations fail to contribute to *yishuvo shel olam* and even invalidated their testimony in court.[12] Developing new products and working in a service profession would be considered examples of work that contributes to society. On the other hand, a person who relies entirely on gambling to earn his livelihood does not contribute positively to society; he is not likely to be a law-abiding citizen; he may lack fear of
G-d;[13] he is a quasi-thief,[14] and
he therefore cannot play any
role in the judicial system as a

> *A person should aim to contribute positively to society.*

witness or judge. By disqualifying such people from the judicial system, the Sages are indicating their disapproval of those who do not contribute to society.

Off Limits

"These shall you abominate." (Vayikra 11:13)

There are certain commercial activities that are inherently forbidden to Jews. For example, not only does the Torah prohibit the eating of certain foods, such as
non-kosher animals and
kosher animals that
were not properly
slaughtered, it forbids
trading these items as
well.[15] In addition, a

> *Some occupations are off-limits. These include trading in food materials prohibited by Biblical injunction and businesses that provide others the opportunity to sin.*

person may not trade items that one may not derive benefit from, such as *chametz* during the Passover festival.

A Jew is similarly restricted from business activities that provide the opportunity for others to sin, as this violates the biblical injunction of "putting a stumbling block before the blind."[16] Thus, it is forbidden to sell weapons to people who are dangerous or menaces to society.[17] Aside from the need to avoid sin in one's own vocation, a person must also avoid assisting others in sin.

Clean and Easy

"A man should teach his son a trade that is clean and easy." (Kiddushin 82a)

Although the Sages did not tell people which profession they should enter, they did provide some general guidelines:

- First and foremost, one's vocation must allow for the study of Torah.
- Secondly, the Sages advised that one choose a vocation that is *naki* (clean), one that will not lead to or facilitate sin. Along these lines, they instructed, "Do not teach your son a trade in which he will have to work closely with women."[18]
- Moreover, the vocation should be *kal* (easy); it should not be one that will not drain a person physically and mentally so that he has little energy left for Torah.

The Sages related to each situation on an individual basis. In some cases, in which there was a concern for immoral behavior, they prohibited a person from entering that field. For example, while the Talmud considers work as a tailor to be "clean and easy," it can be spiritually harmful if he designs and makes woman's clothing. Similarly, an unmarried man should not teach elementary school children, as this could bring him in close contact with their mothers.[19] In other cases, the Sages simply cautioned the person before choosing a specific field. Thus, Abba Guryan is cited by the Talmud as advising people not to apprentice their children in trades that he felt led to various forms of theft. (In those days this included various forms of a carriage drivers and freight haulers. It also included shepherds and shopkeepers.)[20] In these instances, the problem is not the profession itself, as in the case of trading forbidden items, but rather the particular circumstances in which the profession might lead to spiritual danger.

Earning a living is never an excuse or justification for immoral behavior. Before taking any position, men and women must consider how it may impact their morality. Each person must know his own weaknesses and vulnerabilities; if he feels that a specific venue will cause him to sin, he should not enter that field. At the same time, the fact that commercial activity by its nature entails the risk of sin does not, in and of itself, justify avoiding participation in *some* form of livelihood. In fact, *Chovos HaLevavos* explains that one of the reasons man must work is to see if he will follow the ways of G-d or rebel against them.[21] Consequently,

> *A person must avoid occupations that create circumstances which may lead to immoral behavior.*

earning a livelihood naturally involves challenges, and failure to do so can result in sin. The Sages were trying to prevent *additional* sin that is not inherent in commercial activity or labor.

Close to the Government

"Beware of the rulers, for they befriend someone only for their own benefit." (Avos 2:3)

The Sages cautioned people against accepting positions that would bring them too close to the government. Here too, the concern is for one's spiritual growth and Torah observance. In particular, the Sages were concerned that once a person becomes close with the powers of government, be it local or national, his devotion to the government will grow to the detriment of his devotion to G-d and His Torah. This occurs when a person becomes so dedicated to and focused on his government service that his performance of mitzvos weakens. The yoke of government can supplant the absolute sovereignty of G-d that should permeate a person's life.[22] It is not working for the government, per se, that is of concern; rather it is the risk that working closely with the government could dominate a person's life. Indeed, Don Yitzchak Abarbanel, who was in close contact with the king's court his entire life, attests that this experience was detrimental to his personal growth.[23]

> *Service and devotion to large and powerful institutions can often be of detriment to the service of G-d. This is relevant to governments as well as large corporations.*

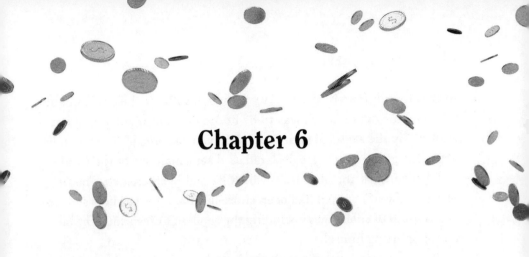

Chapter 6

Attitudes toward Livelihood

While work in some form is clearly necessary to maintain financial self-sufficiency, what is less clear is the appropriate attitude toward this work.

On the one hand, work can be seen as a necessary evil: inherently mundane occupations that help man survive in the physical world of his existence but without profound purpose. On the other hand, the very fact that work bestows man with the means to support himself is noteworthy. This alone lends a sense of importance that should shape man's attitude toward his livelihood. A person's outlook toward his livelihood is significant; it will form his approach, and ultimately his actions toward it. It may even affect his view of his entire financial life. This section will look at the Sages' attitude about work.

Work and Creation

"And the earth was confused and tangled." (Bereishis 1:2)

Before looking at the Sage's attitude toward work, it is worthwhile to look at work in a larger context, namely as a part of the creation of the world and man. After Adam sinned he was punished with, "... through suffering shall you eat of it all the days of your life. Thorns and thistles shall it sprout for you, and you shall eat the herb of the field. By the sweat of your brow shall you eat bread until you return to the ground" (*Bereishis* 3:17–19). Although some of the punishment was only for Adam, much was to be borne by all of mankind; in particular, "By the sweat of your brow shall you eat bread." Immediately after this punishment was declared, G-d sent man out of the Garden of Eden to work the land from which he had been created. The first phase in the life of man had been short-lived and he was now sent to face a world of challenges, including the challenge of working the land and supporting himself.

It is interesting that even prior to Adam's sin there is indication that he would need to work. Just after man was created, it says that G-d put him in the Garden of Eden to "work it and guard it." The simple meaning of this suggests that man was intended to work right from the beginning of creation, even before the sin.[1] Later, after the sin, Adam was punished. This meant that work would now be demanding and its success would only come with difficulty, whereas beforehand it would come with ease.

Others are of the opinion that "to work and guard it" does not refer to working the land. It might refer to protecting the fruit in the garden but not to working the land as a farmer. Alternatively, the subject in the verse is Adam's soul, not the land or garden.[2] According to this approach, there is no reference to man working until after the sin. Whereas before the sin his needs were provided for in the Garden of Eden; afterward, he would have to take care of himself through hard work.

There is, however, another way to understand what happened as a consequence to Adam's sin. This approach combines elements of both these approaches, but differs in that there was no change from before and after the sin. The *Medrash* comments with a parable on the words, "and the earth was *tohu vavohu*," confused and tangled (*Bereishis* 1:2). What was the earth confused and astonished about?

> *It can be compared to a king that acquired two servants with one contract. On one servant the king decreed that he should be fed from the king's treasury, but for the other servant the king decreed that he would have to work to eat. The second servant*

was bewildered: Is this fair? Both servants were purchased with the same contract and for the same value, yet he would have to work and the other one would be taken care of by the king? So too, the earth was confused by the split in creation between the upper world and the lower world. The celestial sphere was to be sustained directly from G-d without any effort, whereas the lower world (man) was created with a need to work in order to eat. The earth saw its lot was not as good as that of the celestial sphere and on this it was confused and tangled, wondering why it was so. (Bereishis Rabbah 2:2)

Rabbeinu Bachya (1255–1340) explains that G-d had already accounted for the sin of man when He created the world. G-d knew man would sin and thus created the world in such a way that man would have to toil to earn a living.[3] Thus, the *Medrash* says the world was created with the inherent need for man to work in order to provide for himself; the alternative would have left man in a dangerous moral position. If his needs were taken care of without effort, man would abuse his free time and rebel against G-d. The antidote to this problem was to require him to engage in self-support.[4]

The challenge of man is to recognize G-d and His role in providing for man. Had man been provided with his needs, he would have failed to see G-d's role. Once man was charged to provide for himself, it remains his primary purpose to see the Hand of G-d in all that he does — despite man's own role. This is not an easy task, and the Torah itself warns of the problem, "and you will raise your heart and forget G-d" (*Devarim* 8:14). Eating leads to satiation, and satiation of physical needs lead man astray. It is not only physical satiation but the abundance of wealth that fosters this problem, as the previous verse says, "and your cattle and flocks will increase, silver and gold will be increased to you!"

Therein lies a risk — but also an opportunity. The risk is that man might indeed lose sight of G-d's role in providing for him. The opportunity arises, however, for man to engage in self-support with the appropriate perspective and recognition that it is a partnership. Success in this area enables man to achieve great heights, as he fosters his relationship with G-d by seeing His role in all aspects of life, even those in which it might appear that man was the only player.

Love Work

"Love work." (*Avos 1:10*)

Given the Sages' view that one must make an effort to support himself in order to enable his Torah learning and other honorable activities, it might be expected that the Sages would view work as a necessary evil.[5] This is especially so if the fundamental need for man to work and the value of maintaining financial self-sufficiency is as means of preventing a person from sinning and rebelling against G-d.[6]

Nevertheless, Shlomo Hamelech speaks quite highly of the value of work and industriousness in *Mishlei*, "Have you seen a man with alacrity in his work? He will stand before kings" (*Mishlei* 22:29), and "but the hand of the diligent brings prosperity" (*Mishlei* 10:4). The Sages similarly espoused an overwhelmingly positive perspective on work, going so far as to instruct their students to "love work." Why did they view work positively, when it seems to be nothing more than a necessary means to achieve loftier goals?

One possibility is that the Sages were instructing their students to appreciate the value of the work that people are compelled to do. As seen previously, the Sages insisted that a person make the effort to support himself, even if this entails taking a job that he perceives as beneath his dignity. Nonetheless, he is told to "love work," as it spares him from the embarrassment and pain that faces those who cannot take care of themselves.[7] The Sages do not charge their followers to "do" work, but to "love it." A person should not do it begrudgingly, as if under duress, but rather with love and joy. Obviously, this is significantly easier if one finds work that matches his personality and talents. A person who does what he loves will perform his tasks with ease and will be more productive.[8]

Work should be done with love and joy.

Giving It Your All

"The man became exceedingly prosperous." (Bereishis 30:43)

One of the greatest examples of an individual who worked with great diligence is Yaakov, who worked for his father-in-law, Lavan, for twenty years. Despite the fact that his employer was woefully dishonest, exchanging Leah for Rachel without Yaakov's knowledge and switching Yaakov's wages again and again, Yaakov worked with great integrity, even doing more than was required of him (*Bereishis* 31:6). He gave of himself to such an extent that he commented, "By day scorching heat consumed me, and frost by night. My sleep drifted from my eyes" (*Bereishis* 31:40).

Rambam writes that just as an employer must be careful to pay his employees, an employee must be careful not to steal his work time from the employer, rather he should put his full effort into his work.[9] For this reason, Rambam refers to Yaakov as a *tzaddik*, as he put all of his energy into his work for Lavan. A righteous person not only works, but gives it his all.

Rambam concludes that Yaakov was rewarded for his hard work not only in the next world, but in this world as well.[10] Apparently, it is obvious that such upright conduct warrants great reward in the next world. What is less obvious is the reward in this world, and Rambam therefore makes a point that Yaakov was rewarded in this world as well. While working as a shepherd is seemingly mundane, Yaakov used his work as a means of serving G-d; he was therefore rewarded in both worlds. Clearly, hard work can have great consequences when performed with the correct intentions.

The power and merit of honest work is also brought out by another statement the Sages made regarding Yaakov's work for Lavan. The Torah says, "Had not the G-d of my father Avraham and the sacred awe at the offering of Yitzchak been for me, you would have now sent me away empty. G-d saw my wretchedness and the labor of my hands and He proved it last night" (*Bereishis* 31:42).[11] The *Medrash* comments on this verse that the work of one's hands has a greater power than the merit of the fathers (Avraham and Yitzchak) and is more beloved before G-d. Yaakov indicates that while the merit of his fathers served to save his property (his father-in-law would have sent him away empty-handed), it was the merit of his own work that saved lives.[12]

How is it that the merit of his work had a greater impact than the merit of his fathers, who had lived long lives and excelled in the service of G-d? Work benefits the person by providing a means for living and preventing any need for theft or other forms of ill-gotten means. The merit of providing this for oneself is immeasurable. The merit of Avraham and Yitzchak (as well as Yaakov) extends millennium beyond their own lives, and yet the merit of providing a livelihood is still greater for the one who has provided for himself and family. It is a personal merit which recognizes the importance of caring for one's physical needs and taking precaution to avoiding illicit gains.

Based on this, the *Medrash Tanchuma* draws the following conclusion:

> *A person should not say, "I will eat and drink and enjoy good things and not bother myself to work and Heaven will have mercy on me." Rather a person needs to toil and work with his two hands and the Holy One will send His blessing.*

The message of the Sages is clear: There is something inherently valuable in work and self-sufficiency. Its value is, in a sense, spiritual, since it can be compared to — and even surpasses — the merit of Avraham and Yitzchak.

Work has a tremendous value and can bring great merit to the one who does it.

For work to reach this level, it needs to be elevated to the point where it represents service to G-d. While the activity a person engages in may be mundane in and of itself, it is the intent that raises his endeavors to a different sphere. This concept is alluded to in the Torah's command regarding the Sabbath: "Six days shall you work and accomplish all your work; but the seventh day is Sabbath for the Lord your G-d; you shall not do any work" (*Shemos* 20:9–10).

Rambam suggests one way of understanding this verse is that for six days, man serves G-d by doing his work, thus, "six days shall you work;" the work itself constitutes service to G-d. This is so when it is done "for the sake of Heaven," in accordance with the precepts of the Torah and with the proper intentions. With the correct intentions, ordinary activities can be elevated to the status of *avodah* (service of G-d). The Sabbath, in contrast to the six days, is for focused devotion to G-d, in the absence of work.[13] Work done on this level has the power to generate tremendous merit for its doer since it is a form of service.

The Evils of Idleness

"Idleness leads to craziness." (*Kesuvos* 59b)

Some of the commentators explain that work is an inherently positive value because it combats the evils of idleness.[14] When a person is idle, it can lead him into all sorts of trouble. Indeed, too much free time can lead to overindulgence in physical pleasures that can ultimately lead to the rejection of G-d, as the Torah states, "Yeshurun became fat and kicked [at G-d]...and it deserted G-d, its maker" (*Devarim* 32:15). The absence of the need to pursue a livelihood can put a person in a place of true spiritual danger, because by his very nature, man tends to rebel against G-d when he is not occupied with tending to his physical needs. When the Sages said to "love work," they were even speaking to people who have sufficient means so that they need not work. Nonetheless, even people of such means should have some form of work, as too much idle time will only lead to spiritual ruin.[15]

It is in this vein that the Sages teach that one should be involved both in the study of Torah and in work, as effort in both realms is necessary to prevent sin. Each has its role in removing a person's evil inclination, and together they keep a person busy, hence keeping him out of trouble.[16] The *Medrash* comments about Adam that after being created he was not permitted to eat until he had done some work, thus demonstrating the crucial role of work in the life of mankind.[17] This was necessary even though all of his needs were provided for him.

One lesson that can be taken is that work enables people to contribute to the physical world from which they derive benefit. It is inappropriate for man to only be a taker; he must also be a giver.[18] *Avos D'Rabi Nosson* goes further and states that just as the Torah was given with a treaty, so to work was given with a treaty, indicating that work has mitzvah-like qualities.[19] Although essentially mundane, work possess qualities that prevent sin and other troubles from finding man, making it an essential part of human life.

Others understand that the Sages' adage, "Love Work," is speaking to the majority of people — those who must work to support themselves. They should love work because it provides them with sustenance, removes the need to steal, and precludes embarrassment that might ensue were they in need of assistance from others.[20] It also prevents them from being idle and avoids all the troubles that this entails. It would follow from this that if a person is financially independent and can engage in Torah study on a full time basis so that he would not be idle, then there would be no need to work.[21]

> *Both work and Torah are necessary, as each plays a role in averting man from sin.*

For some people, idleness may lead to associating with negative elements of society that can influence them to sin. Work, on the other hand, helps to prevent these associations. Thus, "He who works his land will be satisfied with bread, and one who pursues empty people is lacking intelligence."[22] In other words, one who works is rewarded with satiation, while one who due to his idleness, falls in with those who do not contribute to society is unwise. Work provides more than just monetary support; it also maintains intelligence and mental well-being while keeping man away from those who might turn him away from the proper path.[23]

The Sages' view of idleness as evil is reflected in domestic life as well. The Sages mandated that even if a couple is extremely wealthy and can afford to have all of their household needs performed by others, the woman of the house must still actively contribute to the upkeep of the home to some degree. The Sages were concerned that the woman's idleness would lead to evil — either sin or mental illness.[24] Too much idle time is dangerous to one's spiritual and mental health. Of course, these dangers of idleness are by no means limited to a woman in her home! Thus, the Sages taught to love work. Involvement in activities that contribute to society help maintain a healthy emotional balance.[25]

The prophet Yeshayah describes the effects of idleness on the spiritual well-being of the nation as a whole: "There are harp and lyre and drum and flute and wine at their drinking parties, but they would not contemplate the deed of G-d and would not look at the work of His hands" (*Yeshayah* 5:12). The leisure class in Yeshayah's time chose to spend their time indulging in parties and drink, instead of studying Torah and contemplating G-d's handiwork. They abused their free time, and the results were catastrophic; their indolence eventually led to the exile.[26]

The evils of idleness are further portrayed in *Mishlei*: "The lust of the sluggard will kill him; for his hands refuse to work. All day long he will court lust, but a righteous person gives and does not hold back."[27] This verse offers an interesting comparison between the lazy person, who refuses to work and has endless desires, and the righteous person. The

Avoiding idleness keeps many evils away from a person as well as helping to maintain his spiritual vitality.

implication is that a righteous person is not lazy; rather he is the opposite — he lives life with vigor and great energy. While piety is usually associated with the meticulous performance of mitzvos and extra care in avoiding sin, behind these actions are character traits. One of the defining qualities of the *tzaddik* is his energy. What does righteousness have to do with not being lazy? Unlike the lazy person, the *tzaddik* does not want to rely on others. He cannot be lazy because he wants to support himself. Righteous people want to be givers, not takers, and they therefore remove any trace of laziness from their being.[28] Idleness has no place in the life of a *tzaddik*.

The Fruits of Your Labor

"The fruit of the days are the nights; the fruit of the week is the Sabbath." (Kuzari 3:5)[29]

Man can become so occupied with earning a living and a multitude of other daily tasks that he may easily lose sight of *why* he is doing it all. What is he trying to accomplish? What are the "fruits" that man wishes to produce?

The Meiri (1249–1306) explains that days prepare for the night; work during the day enables man to study Torah and meditate on its teachings at night. Similarly, man works during the week so that he can

Physical endeavors should promote spiritual pursuits.

rest on the Sabbath. This rest is not simply about ceasing from proscribed labors (*melachah*), but it is a time for contemplation and the study of Torah. Thus, the fruit of the week is the Sabbath.[30] The focus of all physical endeavors is guided toward producing spiritual fruit — time that can be devoted to spiritual endeavors.

Perspective and Balance

"Man goes forth to his work and to his labor until the evening." (Tehillim 104:23)

While the purpose of wealth is to serve as a tool to facilitate the pursuit of higher goals in this world, it can easily become a distraction. The acquisition of wealth takes time, effort, and energy. When man invests these resources into the acquisition of wealth, he can easily be sucked into a world in which there are no limits to the pursuit of monetary success. When he continues to put in additional time and effort beyond his actual needs, he enters a spiritually dangerous area that can leave him without sufficient time to pursue higher goals.

For this reason, the Sages taught, "Limit your business activities and occupy yourself with Torah,"[31] and "Not all who increase in commercial activity become wise."[32] Although the Sages felt that it is crucial to find a means of self-sufficiency, they stressed that one's primary activity should be Torah study. Commercial activity taxes the mind and thereby limits one's capacity to learn Torah during his study time. By limiting one's commercial activities to that which is absolutely necessary, one reserves his energies for his higher goals and endeavors. Essentially, the Sages warned not to become so consumed by work that little time remains for more important pursuits.[33]

In today's world, with the Internet, constant emails, and other modes of communication, it is easy to become caught up in the pursuit of wealth, working around the clock in pursuit of a livelihood that can quickly dominate a person's life. As a result, a person is unable to focus on more essential goals. His time for Torah study, contemplation, and the pursuit of wisdom becomes severely limited.

> *The Sages warned not to become so consumed by work that little time remains for more important pursuits.*

Consequently, a person's entire worldview becomes distorted, as it is only through Torah that he can maintain a clear picture of his obligations in this world. If, due to one's mundane pursuits, he has no time for Torah study, he will lack a clear understanding of his purpose in this world. Without this clarity his character development will suffer, along with his performance of mitzvos.[34]

The acquisition of wisdom and the development of character take a great deal of time. Wisdom cannot be acquired in a haphazard fashion; it requires dedication and commitment. If the drive for worldly pleasures is not curtailed, it can become all-consuming, and a person's spiritual side will be left wanting. Thus, while a person must take considerable steps to help ensure economic self-sufficiency, he must also be vigilant that his desire for wealth does not overtake him.

While the Sages were wary of a person becoming overly engrossed in his business pursuits, they were particularly concerned for those who must travel to earn a livelihood. They interpret the verse, "Nor is it across the sea" (*Devarim* 30:13), as teaching that Torah cannot be found among traveling merchants.[35] The reason is fairly obvious; it is not necessary to elaborate on the challenges that any person faces if he wants to study when traveling. Even today, despite the many conveniences available, the study of Torah while traveling remains a challenge. Rabbi Baruch Epstein (1860–1941) notes that it can be inferred from the Sages' statement that they would recommend choosing a business that allows a person to stay at home, or at least work in the vicinity of his home. This is a better environment for earning a livelihood and to facilitate the study of Torah.[36]

Nevertheless, although it is difficult to maintain Torah learning while traveling, it is not impossible. Perhaps it is for this reason that the Sages taught that "not all" who increase their commercial activity become wise; allowing room for exception.[37] Even so, the study of Torah is difficult under these circumstances and does not allow for the full development of the scholar, as his studies will likely not be on a level that will help make him wise.

Extensive travel can be harmful to growth in Torah.

Recognizing that there must be an appropriate balance between work and Torah study has far-reaching consequences, in particular when choosing a livelihood. Some forms of support require greater investment of time and energy, and take more out of the person. The more a person gives of himself to his work, the less time will remain to serve G-d. Consequently, care must be taken when choosing a means of support; it should not distract from more fundamental goals.[38]

A person must find a balance between work and the study of Torah so that his work does not overcome his Torah.

Where Does It All Come From?

"You shall remember G-d, that it was He who gave you strength to make wealth." (Devarim 8:18)

What can a person do to ensure that he maintains the proper perspective in his pursuit of a livelihood while he navigates the hustle and bustle of this world? How does a person keep sight of his values?

One suggestion is to consider this very question while engaged in his livelihood. In other words, while engaged in work he should contemplate why he is doing what it is that he might be doing and what its ultimate purpose is. The Meiri explains that this is one way to understand the Sages' statement, "Lead them in the ways of the world:"[39]

> *Let them contemplate when they do their work. When they gather in their crops and fruit, they should consider the significance of accumulating wealth and the future of man. These thoughts will cause him to realize that his fruits are not that important, and this will lead him to pursue wisdom and that which is eternal.*[40]

Another less philosophical approach is that while engaged in work, a person should recognize that he is occupied with providing for his needs and the needs of his family with the purpose of once again immersing himself into Torah. This keeps his work focused on its ultimate purpose and can help prevent him from being pulled into pursuing more than he needs.[41]

Chapter 7

Spending

When it comes to financial independence, income-producing activities are only one part of the equation. Equally as important is how the income is spent. No matter how much a person earns, if he continues to spend more than he earns, over time he will be unable to maintain financial self-sufficiency. Spending habits thus play a crucial role in establishing financial self-sufficiency. Additionally, other questions must be considered when it comes to spending and using wealth.

Wealth, in any form, is a resource granted by G-d to man. The Sages teach that it should be viewed as if G-d has given something to man to take care of on His behalf; man is merely a custodian of the wealth with which he has been blessed. Consequently, there are limitations on how it should be used, since on the most fundamental level it does not belong to its possessor. What are some of the limits placed on how wealth is used? Furthermore, how a person spends his money can have an impact on his own personality and on those around him. This is an area that requires sensitivity, as often the issue is not the purchase itself but the intent behind it. This section will look at the Sages' teachings regarding spending and utilization of wealth.

Living within One's Means

"Good is the man who is gracious and lends,
who conducts his affairs with justice." (Tehillim 112:5)

The Talmud explains that a man who "conducts his affairs with justice" refers to one who understands his needs and takes care of them according to his means.[1] He does not attempt to satisfy all of his heart's desires, but is satisfied that he is provided with his needs.[2] Spending beyond one's means is wasteful and unnecessary, demanding additional time and effort that would be better spent in service of G-d.[3]

The Sages note that there are varying guidelines regarding spending. For example, one should eat less than his means allow for, both in order to preserve his finances and in order to conquer his desires. Nevertheless, he should provide his family with food in accordance with his means.[4] Although he should provide for them according to his means, it is not necessary for a person to overextend himself in order to provide his family with the best of everything the world offers. When it comes to clothing, the middle path is appropriate. A Jew must make the effort to look presentable, and should therefore provide himself clothing according to his means. If one spends too little on clothing, he will lose self-respect; if he spends too much, he will become haughty.

Interestingly, the Talmud instructs that a person should try to honor his family, in particular his wife, (just) beyond his means.[5] One aspect of maintaining peace in the home is ensuring that his family has what they need — and then some. In addition, if a man shows concern and compassion for his family — those who are dependent on him — then measure-for-measure the Almighty will provide the same for him, as he is dependent on the Creator.[6]

> *There are varying guidelines toward spending, but the underlying rule is to spend only within one's means.*

If spending is determined by personal resources, it follows that the spending habits of the wealthy, the poor, and the middle class are going to be different. The wealthy, for example, can afford to eat meat regularly, while the poor have to make do with substitutes. Spending habits should be determined by what one has and what one earns.[7]

The *Sefer HaChinuch* (thirteenth-century Spain) explains that the Torah alludes to this idea when delineating the sacrifice known as *korban oleh veyored*, an offering whose value varies depending on the financial status of the one bringing it.[8] Each person should bring a sacrifice that is of the appropriate value for him. According to the *Sefer HaChinuch*, a poor person cannot bring the sacrifice that a rich person brings because a person should not spend beyond his means.[9]

Financial choices must be based not only on the present situation, but also on the realistic future. Sometimes, it is preferable for a person

> *It is better to owe a small amount of money now than a greater amount in the future.*

to spend beyond his means today to help prevent problems from developing in the future. For example, if a person requires a specific diet to protect his health, if necessary, he should borrow money in order to afford it. He must, in this instance, spend beyond his present means because failure to improve his health now may very well lead to greater problems in the future. Thus, borrowing a small amount in the present may prevent an even greater reliance on others in the future.[10]

Budgets

"One who can eat bread made from barley but eats bread made from wheat violates the prohibition of wasting his possessions." (Shabbos 140b)

Every individual must make sure that his expenses are in line with his income. Rav Chisda commented that if a person can eat barley bread but eats wheat instead, he is in violation of wasting his possessions. Rav Pappa echoed this idea and said the same is true if a person can drink beer but instead drinks wine. Apparently, they viewed eating better and more expensive food as unnecessary and imprudent.[11] The Talmud rejects this, saying that taking care of the body is also important, and thus eating higher quality food is justified.[12] Nonetheless, the basic concept is clear when it comes to spending: Even the most basic needs might need to be limited in order not to spend more than one has.[13] To further illustrate this idea, Rav Chisda commented that when he was poor, he would not eat vegetables, as this would whet his appetite and he simply could not afford to eat more. This is just one example the Sages offered to illustrate how a person can take small steps to reduce his spending. At the same time, Rav Chisda commented that later when he became wealthy he did not bother with vegetables since he could afford meat. When a person has the means, it is not necessary to limit what he eats based on the cost.

For the Sages, it was a given that one's personal spending must be within his means. As such, when challenged to maintain a balanced budget, a person must take corrective action. This includes increasing income and curtailing spending. Even daily bread can be subject to cuts if required. Spending beyond what a person can truly afford is an untenable situation.

Spending should not exceed income.

Creating a Budget

"One's sustenance is set between Rosh Hashanah and Yom Kippur." (Beitzah 16a)

The Sages state that every year, during the Ten Days of Repentance, a person's yearly income — with the exceptions of funds needed for the Sabbath and holidays and to teach one's children — is set. Rashi notes an important implication of this statement:

> All that he will profit in the coming year is set; he will earn such and such. And he should be careful not to spend too much, as he will not have any additional income.[14]

In other words, since income is fixed, a person needs to be careful how he spends what he has. If he spends too much, he may have insufficient funds for the year. Consequently, he needs to be mindful of both his income and his expenses — and budget appropriately.

Budgeting is not only for those with small incomes. The wealthy can also spend beyond their income. In fact, wealth can directly lead to poverty if its possessor is not careful about how he spends it; more than a few millionaires and lottery winners have ended up with nothing.[15] The habit of overspending on pleasures leads not only to poverty but also to other destructive habits, such as laziness.[16]

> *Budgeting and care with expenditures are crucial for financial stability.*

Holiday Spending

"Everyone according to what he can give, according to the blessing that G-d gives you." (Devarim 16:17)

There are occasions when the Torah encourages — and even mandates — that people enjoy some of the physical pleasures of this world. The holidays are one such example, as they obligate the people to rejoice in the day with festive meals of meat and wine. While the mitzvah of rejoicing in the holidays includes physical pleasures, the command is to rejoice in a way that serves G-d. Intoxication and the giving over of ourselves to merrymaking are the antithesis of serving G-d; these have no part in the holiday celebrations.[17] While food and drink are to be used in celebrating the holidays, it is always in moderation and with a distinct purpose, namely a rejoicing that serves G-d. The outward rejoicing on these days through bodily enjoyments is a reflection of the more fundamental command to rejoice on these days in the heart. Internal happiness certainly does not find its expression in wildness and intoxication.

The idea of spending within a person's means is relevant even when he is obligated to spend. *Halachah* mandates that a man provide his family members with something special to enjoy on every holiday, but this is to be done in accordance with his means.[18] Similarly, one should have nicer clothing for the festivals than for the Sabbath, but only if one can afford it.[19] The Sages did not suggest that one buy on credit in order to buy nicer clothing, although such a concept does exist with respect to food for the Sabbath and holidays.[20] Instead, they advised to spend according to one's means. Spending more money than one can afford was untenable to the Sages.

> *The Sages instructed people not to spend more than they can afford even for the holidays.*

Spending for Pleasure

"A lover of pleasure will be a man who lacks." (Mishlei 21:17)

The prophets reproached the Jewish People for adopting a hedonistic approach to life.[21] The Torah teaches man to stay clear of this attitude for many reasons. On the most fundamental level, a person who lives for the pursuit of pleasure demonstrates that he does not understand the purpose of man in this world. He is focused on deriving enjoyment from this world's pleasures, instead of deriving pleasure from serving G-d. On a practical level, a life of excessive indulgence can quickly lead a person to poverty, as he squanders his wealth and becomes slothful and indolent.[22] Simply put, monetary reasons should be sufficient to keep him from this path: "The lover of wine and oil will not grow rich" (*Mishlei* 21:17).[23]

> *A life of excess can lead to poverty.*

Spending for Happiness

"One who is seduced by his wine is agreeable to his maker!" (Eiruvin 65a)

While the Sages teach that a person should not pursue the enjoyments of this world for their own sake, on some occasions this might be appropriate. The key is to always be sensitive to intent. Sometimes, a person needs things — such as a home, food, or other mundane items — to help maintain a sense of happiness. Often, people are unable to generate feelings of happiness internally and require an external stimulus to help restore positive feelings. Examples of this may be the need to beautify a home or perhaps take a vacation. If the intent is appropriate, then these indulgences are also appropriate.

This is what the Sages meant when they said a drinker is "agreeable to his maker." The Meiri explains:

> *Although a person must be careful not to pursue the pleasures of this world, still, if he does this with a noble intent such as to maintain his happiness so that his mind will be clear, not for the purpose of pleasure alone, such a person should be blessed.*[24]

The Sages taught to always act for the sake of Heaven. This means that a person should look to uplift all of his thoughts and actions to the point where they are focused on serving G-d. A person who conducts himself at this level eats not because the food tastes good, but in order to provide energy for his body to serve G-d. Similarly, such a person goes to sleep in order to recharge and reinvigorate his body to serve G-d. At the highest level, a person who lives his life for the sake of Heaven is not looking to take pleasures from this world, but rather to serve G-d through every means available. He is not focused on himself, but on G-d: All of his activities become a platform for this service.

Spending on pleasure is appropriate when the purpose is noble.

Shlomo Hamelech teaches, "In all of your ways know Him, and He will smooth your paths" (*Mishlei* 3:6). Uplifting the mundane and serving G-d in this way is praiseworthy and merits reward, and it also leads to further success through greater Divine providence.

Buy the Truth

"Buy truth and do not sell it." (Mishlei 23:23)

One of the most appropriate things to do with wealth is to exchange it for something of much greater value: wisdom. When a person uses wealth to acquire wisdom — by paying a teacher, for example — he has invested in personal growth and perfection, which have eternal value. He exchanges that which is external to his being for that which becomes part of his essence.[25] Through this exchange he obtains knowledge and understanding of the truth, which is the meaning of "buy truth!" This verse, however, concludes with a warning: "and don't sell it." How does a person sell the truth?

While a person cannot literally sell and give up truth that he has already acquired, he can fail to take advantage of opportunities to acquire wisdom. When Shlomo Hamelech warns not to sell the truth, he is referring to those opportunities in which a person gives up time for wisdom and exchanges it to engage in commercial activity.[26] In effect, it is a sale of time.[27] When this type of exchange occurs, instead of advancing a person's spirituality, wealth and physical pursuits become a diversion and interfere with one's primary purpose in this world. Moreover, this practice is likely to leave a person with a befuddled perspective on life, since he has sacrificed time that was to be used for spiritual growth. Consequently, his development as a person and a Torah personality will suffer. While he may continue to observe the basic precepts of the Torah, he certainly will not grow in his service of G-d.[28]

> *Time and money are the currency for the buying and selling of "truth!"*

Wisdom and spiritual growth cannot be acquired in a haphazard fashion; they demand time and effort, dedication and commitment. Rambam explains that a great deal of man's ultimate reward relates to *de'ah*, or knowledge and understanding of G-d and his Torah.[29] A person who spends all of his time on achieving success in this world will have no time to achieve the ultimate reward in the next. Thus, while a person must take steps to achieve economic self-sufficiency, he must also be vigilant so that his desires for wealth do not overcome him. Wisdom is

> *A person should not trade opportunities to acquire wisdom and spiritual growth for wealth.*

one of the key elements to achieving greatness in service of G-d. It is truly tragic when the pursuit of wealth becomes the reason a person fails to acquire wisdom.

Waste Not

"One who grows lax in his work is also a brother to the master of destruction." (Mishlei 18:9)

One aspect of financial responsibility includes not wasting that with which one has been blessed. The Torah articulates this idea in prohibiting the needless destruction of a fruit-bearing tree: "Do not destroy its trees...for you shall eat from it and not destroy it."[30] According to the Sages, this prohibition is not limited to the case of a fruit tree; even spending money in a wasteful manner is included. Thus, Rabbeinu Yonah writes, "We have been exhorted against spending wastefully, even a *perutah*'s worth."[31]

Wasting economic resources and time is, at best, inappropriate, and in many cases it is prohibited.

This concept is not limited to wasting physical resources, but to wasting time as well. Obviously, an employee is obligated to perform the task that he has been hired to perform and not to waste time. However, this notion also applies when a person works for himself. One who is "lax in his work," wasting his own productive time, is akin to one who destroys his own property.[32]

Character and Spending

"When the yetzer hara [evil inclination] sees a man fixing his eyes, playing with his hair, and positioning himself in a haughty manner, it says, 'He is mine!'"
(Bereishis Rabbah 22:6)

The manner in which a person dresses and presents himself can often foster negative character traits. If he dresses in ornate clothing, it might lead to haughtiness and even licentious behavior under certain conditions. As such, even if elegant clothing and jewelry are within a person's means, he should nevertheless be cautious about the manner in which he dresses.[33]

The fact that what a person purchases can influence his character is relevant whether he is buying clothing, a car, a home, or anything else. A person must take responsibility for his own life and ensure that he does not endanger his own character through his personal possessions.

A person must also consider how his purchases will impact others. Will his acquisition arouse envy and jealousy in those around him? Clearly, there are some things a person needs, irrespective of the possible feelings of others. However, there are other items regarding which he must use wise judgment, as they may be seen as luxurious or flashy, and can invite jealousy.[34]

Furthermore, a person who lives on a very high economic standard becomes accustomed to certain comforts and luxuries. These may even become necessities, such that it becomes difficult to live without them. He will then be compelled to spend more time and energy acquiring wealth in order to maintain his standard of living. One of the early scholars interpreted the verse, "G-d made man upright but they have sought out many intrigues" (*Koheles* 7:29), in this light. In other words, man was created with the ability to pursue noble purposes (which include his true needs), but he can lose sight of this by pursuing things which he does not really need but sees as necessities.[35] Man does this to himself, and in doing so he makes crooked that which was created straight.

Keeping one's desires in check enables a person to maintain his standard of living and prevents him from acquiring many unnecessary items. The more successful a person is in this endeavor the more he will grow spiritually.

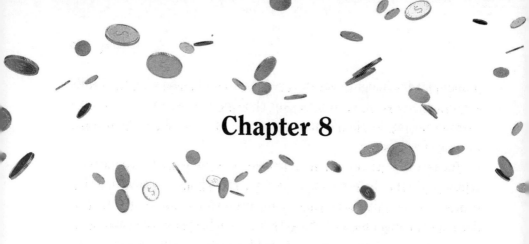

Chapter 8

Financial Planning

Good financial health does not occur by accident. It requires planning and action on both the income side and the expense side of a person's financial life. The Sages were not financial advisors and therefore do not offer specific advice about how to manage personal finances. Indeed, such a proposition would be impossible, as each person has his own unique set of circumstances that makes such counsel foolish. Furthermore, each generation and location is different, making guidance rendered at a specific point in time useless for later generations.

Still, although the Sages were not financial advisors, they do provide guidance in the area of finance because financial self-sufficiency was something they strongly encouraged to help man find success in this world. The Sages wanted to help man succeed spiritually in this world, and spiritual success often requires success in the area of personal finance. To be sure, the Sages' definition of success is not measured in terms of great wealth or earnings. Success in the area of finances means that the person is self-supporting and is able to engage in spiritual pursuits. Spiritual pursuits might involve wealth directly, or the wealth might simply provide the support necessary for other more spiritual endeavors. This next section will look at some of the general guidance the Sages provide in the area of financial planning.

Planning for Success

"Prepare your work outside and provide for yourself in the field; then build your house." (Mishlei 24:27)

The Sages read the above verse as guidance in planning for a successful life. The first step is to know the goal.[1] Accordingly the goal is to "build your house" mentioned at the end of the verse.

Once a man has a goal in mind, he can work to achieve it. The first part of the verse notes the necessary steps to achieve the goal; if one wishes to build a home, to marry, and raise a family, then one should first establish a means of support by "work[ing] outside" and "provid[ing] for yourself." Rambam writes: "The approach of wise people is to first establish a means of support, then to acquire a home, and then to marry a wife."[2] Indeed, if one chooses to marry without first establishing a means of support, he will be forced to rely on others and might even resort to theft.[3, 4]

Building a family is the ultimate reflection of independence: "Therefore, a man shall leave his father and mother and cling to his wife, and they shall become one flesh" (*Bereishis* 2:24). The foundation of this independence is a means of financial support. Thus, the preparation for independence (building a house) must include financial self-sufficiency by working and providing for one's self.

When a person sets out on journey, he takes food so that he will be able to eat later, when food might not be available; similarly, a person must plan ahead in the journey of life. Along these lines, the Sages teach that a wise person is one who is *ro'eh es ha-nolad*, who "sees that which is yet to unfold" — he plans for foreseeable situations.[5]

One should make every effort to plan in a manner geared for success, including taking care of financial needs in a logical order. Bezalel, the chief architect and builder of the Mishkan, constructed the Mishkan before building the holy vessels that were to be placed inside it. He understood that although the holy vessels were the purpose of the entire Mishkan, the structure needed to be built first in order to house the vessels.[6] The sequence of one's actions is often crucial for their success.

In a person's economic life, logical and sequential planning is essen-

Establishing a goal and developing a plan to achieve it are critical steps for success.

tial. Planning can include education, developing a means for self-sufficiency, budgeting, investing, and more. A person can never know what life has in store for him, but when he has a plan, it is easier to stay on course or to get back on course should he veer from it.

After teaching about the need for financial planning, Rambam

Planning and sensible action invite blessing from G-d.

quotes the verse, "David was successful in all of his ways, and G-d was with him" (*Shmuel I* 18:14). Ultimately, success depends on G-d blessing man's endeavors; however, it is when he conducts himself reasonably and sensibly that this blessing takes hold, and this usually entails planning.[7]

Estate Planning

"Then it shall be on the day that he causes his sons to inherit whatever will be his ..." (Devarim 21:15)

The Sages teach that a person should not give more than twenty percent of his income to charity, so that he will not become needy himself. It would seem that this concern does not apply after death,

Estate planning is also part of financial planning.

since at that point self-sufficiency is obviously irrelevant. Accordingly, one should be entitled to give as much of his estate to charity as he wishes at the time of his death. In fact, this is one approach expressed in the halachic literature.[8] Others argue that the needs of the deceased person's family are part of his needs. Consequently, it is inappropriate to leave everything to charity, even at the time of death, if one's family could use some of his wealth. According to this position, the correct approach is to leave one's estate to his inheritors, while leaving a generous donation to charity as well.[9]

Retirement

"Go to the ant, you sluggard; see its ways and grow wise...She prepares her food in the summer and stores up her food in the harvest time." (Mishlei 6:6, 8)

Shlomo Hamelech directs man to study the behavior of the ant in order to learn an important lesson in financial planning. The ant works with great energy and efficiency; indeed, it is one of the most industrious creatures on earth. Shlomo Hamelech notes, in particular, a specific behavior of the ant that metaphorically reflects great wisdom. The ant prepares its food in the summertime when provisions are accessible because it instinctively knows that once the winter comes, nothing will be available. It prepares in advance, while the opportunity is there, enabling it to survive the winter.[10]

Similarly, the Sages said once a person becomes older it is more difficult to find sustenance.[11] Their point was to teach about the need to prepare in advance for one's later years when earn-

> *Planning for retirement cannot be ignored, even when it appears to be in the distant future.*

ing a living becomes more challenging.[12] Just as the ant puts away for the winter, a person must prepare for his "golden years." In this way, a person will maintain financial self-sufficiency even after he retires.[13]

Insurance

"Your life will hang in the balance." (Devarim 28:66)

In today's world, insurance is a matter of course in many areas of a person's financial life. Insurance policies are sold for various forms of property, homes, cars, and valuables. Insurance can be taken out to protect against disability and even against the loss of life. Life insurance is usually purchased to replace the income of the one who provides for the financial needs of the family. It is intended to provide for the family left behind, replacing the lost income for years to come.

Does this aspect of planning — the purchasing of life insurance — reflect a lack of trust that G-d will provide even when the person (the provider) is no longer alive? Absolutely not! Rather, it is part of a person's own involvement in providing for his loved ones. Just as a person goes out to work to earn a living and provide for his family, so too he takes steps to provide for them for when he is no longer alive.[14]

Insurance is part of sound financial planning. Life insurance, in particular, helps satisfy an obligation toward loved ones.

The obligation to provide for dependents takes many forms. The underlying assumption is that a person is obligated to provide for dependents and that he may not choose to rely on miracles, nor should they rely on the kindliness of others.

Life insurance provides an additional benefit for the policyholder while still alive. Since he has the policy, he need not work extra hard to create a large emergency fund and inheritance for his family. This will allow for more time to engage in Torah study and devotion to serving G-d.[15]

Investing

"A person should divide his money into thirds: A third in the ground, a third invested in a business, and a third at hand." (Bava Metzia 42)

One of the major components of financial planning is investing. Investing capital can be complicated, as many factors must be considered when determining how to allocate wealth. As such, the Sages did not offer specific advice; rather, they gave broad guidance. Rambam, for example, offers some general principles, but the details of how to invest are left for each individual to determine based on his unique circumstances.

Rambam writes, "A person should place his attention and interest to see that his estate grows...It [wealth] is not for the purpose of fleeting enjoyment or pleasure that brings with it great loss."[16] In other words, a person might grow his assets and wealth, and then waste it rather quickly on various pleasures and enjoyments. This is not the purpose of wealth, and it should not be the purpose of investing.

In accordance with this principle, Rambam writes that a person should not sell a field in order to purchase a home. Fields were viewed as the most valuable possession because they provide food and income, and are permanent in nature — in contrast to homes which are not a source of income.[17] At the same time, a home should not be sold for moveable objects (less permanent) or as a source of cash to fund a business. The permanence of the home is more valuable than what these other opportunities might offer.

The Sages were not satisfied, however, with the creation of a savings account or investing in real estate. Often, a person's trade or business does not provide enough money to live on and additional streams of income are necessary. To make up for this shortfall, the Sages recommended investing a portion of a person's wealth in a business.[18] Classically, this refers to a situation in which a partnership is formed; one person provides funding to purchase merchandise while the active partner buys and sells it, and together they share the profits. Although this is not the typical way that people invest today, the Sages' suggestion indicates their sense that it is necessary to supplement income through investing. Today, purchasing equities could be viewed in a similar way, as the shareholder is a partial owner of the company.

In the twenty-first century, money can be invested in numerous ways, many of which did not exist in earlier times. Each investment vehicle has its own advantages, disadvantages, and unique set of risks and rewards. As stated earlier, Rambam states that the rule here is, "to make one's estate prosper and grow." That can happen only if a person educates himself on how to responsibly invest his wealth.

There are different interpretations of the phrase, "and a third in the ground." One approach is that a person invests part of his assets in land or real estate. Real estate has the advantage of permanence — even better than placing one's money in the ground is to *own* the ground![19]

According to this, the Sages were giving a more direct piece of financial advice. (For an alternative approach, see section titled "Emergency Funds.")

Finally, the Sages advised that a third of one's assets should be "at hand." This phrase refers to liquid assets, such as cash on hand or money that can be accessed quickly if a good business opportunity should arise. In other words, a person should maintain some reserves for opportunities that may present themselves.

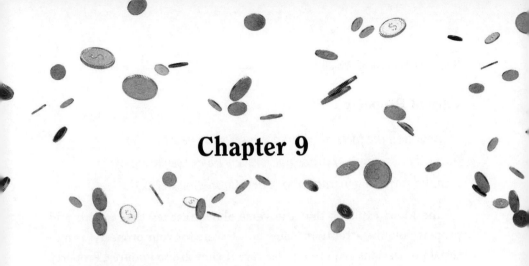

Chapter 9

Wealth Preservation

"Do not love sleep lest you become impoverished; open your eyes and you will be satisfied with food." (Mishlei 20:13)

One of the critical areas of financial planning is managing cash flow, the proper balance between income and expenses. Even someone who has a large income should be careful with his spending to be sure his wealth does not slip through his fingers and leave him with little or nothing. Indeed, it is often easier to create wealth than it is to preserve it.

The Hebrew verb *poke'ach*, used in the verse above means "open your eyes," but it also means clever or intelligent. If a person uses his intelligence and creativity to maintain and preserve his wealth, then he will ultimately be satisfied. Making sure that wealth is not squandered is an important part of financial planning and a safeguard against poverty.[1] G-d gives man the ability to support himself by using his mind and body. When a person fails to take steps in this direction and instead chooses to "sleep," he contradicts G-d's will.[2]

It is often easier to create wealth than it is to preserve it.

Care of Property

"Know well the faces of your sheep; set your heart to the flocks. For strength endures not forever. Does the crown of wealth last from generation to generation?" (Mishlei 27:23–27)

The Meiri explains that the verse above teaches that wealth and property require attention. Know how to care for your property, as material possessions require regular care if they are to endure.[3] Property and possessions decay, disappear, and lose value when not tended to properly. Livestock will become sick or die if neglected; they may even walk away. Untended fields may lose their produce or become barren, and buildings demand maintenance and care. If money is invested in equity markets, it needs to be monitored to see if these positions are the appropriate securities to hold.

In the long run, the benefit of guarding personal assets is obvious; a person will not have to replace property as quickly and it will retain its value. The Sages teach that the righteous should have this care for their wealth. Because they care for what they have, the righteous do not have reason to steal or look elsewhere to obtain their needs.[4]

> *Appreciating one's possessions helps protect from coveting and stealing.*

Similarly, the Sages say that if one wants his wealth to disappear, he should hire workers and not watch over them.[5] Negligence causes one's wealth to vanish before his eyes. Wealth is a crown: the finishing touch for the wise person. Although there is no guarantee that the crown will remain, it will surely disappear if neglected.

"Know well the faces of your sheep; set your heart to the flocks. For strength endures not forever. Does the crown of wealth last from generation to generation?" An alternate reading of these verses concludes with a different twist. Since wealth does not last forever, a person must find a way to convert it into eternity. While the development of the soul is everlasting, a "crown" — money — is fleeting and a person must strive to convert it into something with permanence, such as support for the poor. According to this understanding, the message of the verse is to convert transitory wealth into eternity by using it to perform mitzvos.

> *It is always appropriate to use wealth in performing mitzvos and helping others.*

Emergency Funds

"A person should divide his money [and put]... a third in the ground..." (Bava Metzia 42)

One important element of financial planning is the creation of an emergency fund in order to have money accessible in times of unforeseeable need, such as unemployment or medical emergency. The Sages suggested creating such a fund when they counseled to put a third of one's assets "in the ground," which in Talmudic times was the safest place to store silver for safekeeping. Today, an emergency fund can be maintained in various ways so that liquid assets will be accessible in times of need.

The importance of an emergency fund is reflected in *halachah* as well. Rabbi Shabtai HaCohen, better known as the Shach (1622–1663), refers to the development of an emergency fund and its prudence. The *halachah* is that one who is classified as *Toraso umnaso*, literally "his Torah is his profession," is exempt from paying certain communal taxes. The *Shulchan Aruch* defines *Toraso umnaso* as a person who spends most of his time engaged in Torah study and earns only enough income through work to support himself, not to become wealthy.[6] The Shach adds:

> *The words of the Shulchan Aruch do not mean that he may only earn the minimum amount to support himself. It says he is not trying to become wealthy; it does not say he is not trying to earn more than minimal living needs. This is obvious, as things always happen to people, be it illness or other events, and he will need to spend large sums of money. There is no limit to such expenses.*[7]

In other words, emergencies and other life events do arise and an

An emergency fund is a basic part of financial planning.

individual or family must be ready to contend with them. Consequently, there is an actual need to have an emergency fund available and a person must put away funds for this purpose.

Bitachon and Emergency Funds

"Trust in G-d with all your heart, and do not rely on your own understanding." (Mishlei 3:5)

As seen previously, the Sages recognized the need for an emergency fund. How does the concept of an emergency fund fit in with the concept of *bitachon* (trust in G-d)? Does development of such a fund reflect a lack of faith that G-d will help in times of trouble? To answer these questions, it is first necessary to understand what *bitachon* means. While it is beyond the scope of this work to present a complete look at *bitachon*, there is one basic, relevant approach presented in early rabbinic literature.

Bitachon means that while people must make an effort in the pursuit of their livelihood or any other endeavor, they must recognize that the success of their endeavors is in G-d's hands.[8] Success depends upon G-d, not on the efforts, intelligence, or plans of man. For example, the Jewish army certainly includes soldiers and weaponry; however, "Some with chariots, some with horses, but we in the name of our G-d call out."[9] The emphasis is on the calling out to G-d. An army that puts its trust in G-d is distinct. It fights like any other army but with one major difference: It recognizes that its success is by the grace of G-d, not because of its strategies. Such an army recognizes that victory belongs not to man, but to G-d who has the power to grant victory by His might.[10]

When it comes to an emergency fund, it is without a doubt that a person must take prudent measures to protect himself. A person should never rely on miracles in times of need.[11] If he himself has not experienced difficult situations, he need only look around him to see people who are in need. Many of them didn't take precautions that could have helped when difficult times fell upon them, and miracles did not occur for them.

Nonetheless, a person's approach to establishing an emergency fund is no different than seeking a livelihood or any other endeavor. It must be with the recognition that the success of these actions is in G-d's hands. It is there that a person should put his trust.

Although in and of itself an emergency fund does not deny the concept of trust in G-d, if taken to an extreme, it might. If a person develops a feeling that he must accumulate wealth to guarantee security for himself and for his children, this may well reflect a lack of trust in G-d. Such a person believes that the burden of sustenance lies on his shoulders

Emergency funds are necessary as a matter of prudence but trust must always be with G-d.

alone; he fails to appreciate G-d's role. It is only when a person recognizes G-d's role and removes the burden from his shoulders that he can partner with G-d to pursue a livelihood, knowing that it is ultimately G-d's responsibility. This mindset will prevent him from being consumed by the need to provide for himself.[12]

Diversification

"And he divided the people that were with him." (Bereishis 32:9)

The Sages often cited sources for concepts that could otherwise have been discovered through logic. While logic can be compelling, often there is a counter-logic that points toward a flaw in the original thought. Therefore, by bringing a proof, the Sages were indicating that the logic behind a specific position was sound, and was supported by the Torah. One such example is that of asset diversification. This is a basic strategy in which investments are divided among different classes of assets in order to reduce risk. Although there is a natural logic to it, the Sages nonetheless brought a textual proof for this concept. They explain that Yaakov implemented this concept in preparation for his confrontation with his brother Eisav.[13] At that time, Yaakov divided his family into two groups in anticipation of a possible battle with Eisav. He took this action as a precaution. If Eisav would be successful, he would harm only part of Yaakov's family. Similarly, a person should not put all of his money in one place.[14]

Diversification helps to protect one's assets and limit risk by not putting everything into one "basket." Even the best of plans is no guarantee of success; risking everything at one time reflects overconfidence and the view that success is based on man's efforts. In addition to the economic advantages offered by asset diversification by reducing risk, it is also a safeguard from natural human frailties

Diversification protects against uncontrollable circumstances.

that can lend themselves to human error. Further, diversification provides an opportunity to recognize Who truly runs the world, as man does not control the success of his endeavors (which is precisely the reason he needs to diversify). So while diversifying an investment portfolio is a wise step, at the same time it reflects upon man's limits and inability to manipulate the world at large.

Chapter 10

Trust

Trust in G-d, or *bitachon*, as it is known in Hebrew, is a trait that is praised throughout the books of *Tehillim* and *Mishlei*. Indeed, it is one of the basic qualities required for a person to excel in his service of G-d. It is crucial to understand how trust in G-d interacts with the need for man to take action in this world, in particular in the area of livelihood. At first glance, it is possible for a person to view trust in G-d and one's own obligation to act as incompatible. Trust in G-d could be construed to mean that man can rely on G-d and need not take action and responsibility for himself, the opposite of what has been discussed thus far in this book.

This is clearly not the case, as indicated by the source cited earlier. Rather, trust means that man should not view the success of his actions as dependent upon himself. Instead, he should recognize that his success depends on the will of G-d. If G-d wills it, then it will be; if He does not, then it will not come to pass. Man certainly must take action, but it is within a framework of recognizing that only G-d controls the outcome.

Scripture and the Sages were well aware of the conflict that can arise between trust in G-d and the pursuit of livelihood. The next section will look at some of the situations in which this tension can arise.

Excessive Effort

"It is vain for you to rise early, who sit up late, who eat the bread of sorrows; for indeed, He gives His beloved ones restful sleep." (Tehillim 127:2)

The commentators explain that the people described in the psalm above put their trust in their own ability to provide for themselves by working from early morning until late at night. The fruits of their labor come with pain, effort, and worry. The psalmist says that this is all in vain: G-d can provide the same results to those who trust in Him even if they do not put in as much effort.[1] Effort is necessary; in fact, the very next psalm praises one who fears G-d and supports himself through work: "Praiseworthy are all those who fear G-d...If you eat of the labor of your hands, praiseworthy are you and it will be good for you" (Tehillim 128:1–2). Ultimately, however, everything in this world is in G-d's control. Man may plan and prepare and build, but if G-d decrees that success will elude him, nothing will come of man's actions.[2]

These *pesukim* teach not only the importance of trusting in G-d to provide sustenance, but also that *bitachon* brings blessing — blessing that flows from the relationship that has been fostered with G-d. If a person develops his trust in G-d, G-d in turn provides a higher level of Divine providence in his life. As a result, a person who trusts in G-d need not worry about his sustenance, as he knows that with G-d at his side, he can accomplish the same as someone who devotes himself entirely to his livelihood.

> While effort is necessary to earn a livelihood, excessive effort is not.

Burden of Livelihood

"Cast upon G-d your burdens, and He will support you." (Tehillim 55:23)

A number of sources have been cited indicating the importance of working to support oneself, and intuitively man can sense that indolence is not a noble trait.[3] How, then, can the psalmist say "cast upon G-d your burdens," indicating a person can rely on G-d rather than take action himself? The answer lies in understanding the term "burdens" used in the psalm. Casting burdens on G-d does not mean that man refrains from work, but that he partners with G-d. He should pursue a livelihood while casting the burden — the worry and concern that accompany the attempt to be self-sufficient — upon G-d. It is not the actual pursuit of livelihood

> *Trust in G-d relieves man of the burden of being successful, not from work itself.*

that is a burden, but the feeling that the person is responsible for making it work. Trust in G-d relieves man of the burden of being successful, not from work itself.[4]

People often feel that they are responsible for the welfare of their family. They live as is everything rests on their shoulders, as if G-d has very little to do with it. The psalmist teaches that this tremendous burden can be removed by trusting in G-d and by recognizing G-d's role in one's livelihood.[5]

Lesson of the Sukkah

"For I made the Children of Israel dwell in booths when I brought them out..." (Vayikra 23:43)

During the forty years that the Children of Israel wandered in the wilderness, the nation lived under G-d's direct providence, relieved entirely of the burden of self-preservation — "the overwhelming weight of the worry of the struggle of existence."[6] They were then able to recognize that G-d can provide for man even when he lacks the protection of society and the natural world is seemingly against him. The experience in the wilderness taught man not to assign much value to his own skill and ingenuity in his quest to obtain a livelihood. It demonstrated that provision of his needs is a function of G-d's intervention, not of his cleverness and manipulations.[7]

The Torah commands the Jewish nation to dwell in *sukkos* (booths) for seven days as a reminder of the wilderness period and the lessons it teaches. Every year, Jews leave their permanent homes to dwell in temporary *sukkos* and, in a sense, relive the event. By doing so they absorb the timeless message that while man is obligated to provide for himself,

> *The sukkah is a reminder that the provision of man's needs is from G-d.*

G-d ultimately provides for man. Even without a solid roof over his head, man can trust in G-d to help him and protect him.[8]

The holiday of Sukkos falls out during the traditional harvest season, when people are most likely to make the mistake of believing that "it is [their] strength and the power of [their] hand that has provided [them] with this wealth" (*Devarim* 8:17). By commanding this mitzvah in the harvest season, the Torah helps prevent this pitfall by recalling that everything man has accomplished is only thanks to the help of G-d.[9]

Approach of the Foolish

"The desire of the lazy will kill him, for his hands refuse to work." (*Mishlei* 21:25)

The book of *Mishlei* levels harsh criticism against those who are lazy and fail to take care of their basic needs. Ironically, sometimes this laziness may result from a simplistic trust in G-d. A person might believe that it is not necessary to take action to support himself, as G-d will take care of him. While this approach may appear to be pious, in truth it is foolish. It can be compared to a person who jumps off a tall building and thinks, "G-d will take care of me."[10] While G-d does indeed provide for all, He expects people to make the effort necessary to provide for their needs. This idea is borne out in Scripture and later elucidated in rabbinic literature.

Indeed, even in verses that might sound as if G-d will take care of a person's needs without their input, the Sages explain that these verses are meant to be understood differently. The Meiri explains the verse, "Fear G-d, his holy ones, for there is no lack for those that fear him" (*Tehillim* 34:10), to mean that they ("his holy one") should put all of their trust in G-d, not in their own efforts, then they can know that there is no lack for those who fear Him, as G-d will help their efforts find success.[11]

Even those who are most dedicated to G-d must put in effort. Shlomo Hamelech emphasizes that the most appropriate way to take action is to plan and think out what one will do, for he says, "one who approaches a matter with intelligence will find good [success]..." (*Mishlei* 16:20).[12] Even with superior planning, and even when done by those who fear Him, a person should not put his trust in his own efforts but in G-d, as the verse concludes, "and praiseworthy is one who trusts in G-d."[13]

End of Work

"The ravens would bring him bread and meat in the morning and bread and meat in the evening." (Melachim I 17:6)

There is a basis to suggest that man can reach a point at which he is relieved of the need to earn a livelihood. Some understand that the original intent of creation was that man was not intended to work.[14] Even today, when everyone agrees that it is necessary to work either because this was, in fact, the original intent of creation, or because this is a punishment resulting from the sin of Adam, there may exist the possibility that this yoke can be relieved from man; however, this can occur only when a number of conditions are met. Relief from the burden of livelihood requires that a person strengthen his devotion to G-d, resolve to fear and trust Him in all of his interests (both secular and holy), avoid all reprehensible acts, and yearn to obtain growth in personal character. He must also see to it that his free time does not lead to rejection of G-d or toward the evils of idleness, and that he controls his evil inclination and is not enticed by the witcheries of the world.

A person who has achieved and obtained these qualities has removed the need to seek a livelihood because of the two primary reasons that obligate man to work:

- The need to test man to see that he will live in accordance with G-d's law
- To prevent him from going astray with too much free time

Once these reasons are no longer applicable, then such a person could be blessed by G-d so that his livelihood comes without struggle.[15] Note that even in such a case, the person will need to work, but the burden will be lifted and his livelihood will come with ease.[16]

The scenario just presented is true in theory; however, such occurrences are most unusual. While there are some examples of this amongst the prophets,[17] in truth it is extremely unusual even among such great men. Any individual who feels he has met all of these qualifications is mistaken. Should a person decide to rely on his trust in G-d and not to make a genuine effort to support himself, the result of his inaction will almost certainly not be miracles but self-inflicted poverty. Scripture refers to such people as "a generation that is pure in its own eyes, and yet is not washed from its own filthiness."[18]

Some of the sages go even further in criticizing a person who does not support himself based on his righteousness, indicating that his actions are a desecration of G-d's name.[19] When the wicked and non-believer see a person of G-d in a destitute state and in need of their gifts, the honor of Heaven is lowered in their eyes. From their perspective, these "righteous people" are interested in this world, as they seek support and gifts from others to live. How much greater is the desecration if they use the gifts for things that are not true necessities! The truly righteous, in contrast, sanctify G-d's name by refusing to accept gifts from others and trusting in G-d to help their efforts succeed.[20]

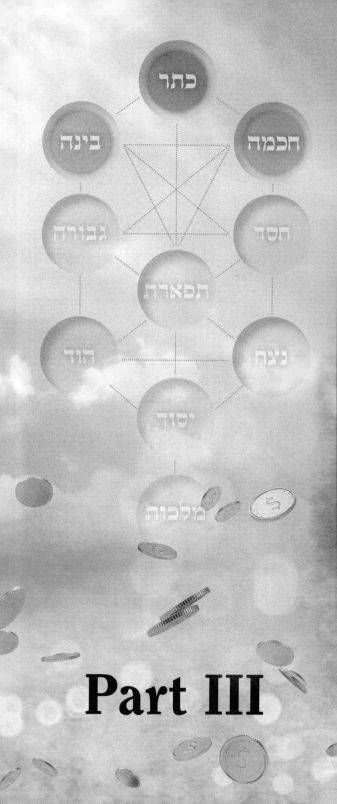

Part III

Wealth
and Poverty

The Sages cautioned people to avoid poverty, as it brings with it a number of problems. Indeed, they taught homiletically that the Torah itself warns to eschew poverty.[1] At the same time, they were well aware of the spiritual dangers that are inherent in wealth. This section will look at some of the concerns.

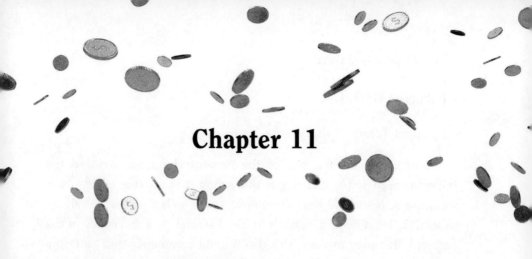

Chapter 11

Problems of Poverty

As indicated in earlier sections, the Sages placed great emphasis on the value of financial self-sufficiency, as reflected in numerous mitzvos and halachos. Consequently, it was necessary for the Sages to encourage an appropriate balance between maintaining self-sufficiency and prioritizing the importance of Torah study. Scripture and the Sages further emphasized the danger of failing to maintain self-sufficiency, reiterating the evils of poverty.

Denial of G-d

"Give me neither poverty or wealth...and lest
I become impoverished and steal, and take the
Name of my G-d [in a vain oath]." (Mishlei 30:8–9)

When poverty becomes severe, the impoverished are at risk to violate many of the commandments, such as stealing or swearing falsely. When one lacks financial means, he risks "cutting corners" and even doing things that are explicitly prohibited. Once a person is in a situation of poverty, there is a greater likelihood of justifying actions that are truly inappropriate.

> *Poverty can test a person's integrity.*

Character Defect

"A pauper utters supplications." (Mishlei 18:23)

As explained earlier, one of the reasons the Sages stressed the importance of self-sufficiency is that when it is missing, a person is incomplete. Some add that when poverty compels a person to rely on others, it also reflects a blemish in his character — a deficiency in the person.[1] This may explain why the Talmud comments that suffering from plagues is preferable to poverty.[2] Plagues are external attacks on the body, while poverty reflects an internal shortcoming. It is better to be a complete person and suffer from external assaults on the body than to be inherently lacking.[3]

In what sense does poverty reflect a flaw in character? Wealth is one factor that influences how a person relates to others. Often, people in one economic class will act differently toward those of another class. For example, a poor person will often speak to others in a supplicating manner and with an element of trepidation, especially if the other person is financially well-off. This is reflected in *Mishlei*: "A pauper utters supplications."[4] It reflects poorly on his character in two ways. First, a person should not have fear of other people and lower himself when speaking with them. Second, his need of others bears shame. Financial self-sufficiency is a remedy to this problem.[5] In addition, self-sufficiency can help a person to develop a sense of self-worth. The Talmud comments that wealth gives a person standing.[6]

> *Although a person's intrinsic value has nothing to do with money, money can often help create a feeling of self-worth.*

In other words, it gives its owner importance. Similarly, Rashi explains, "when the famine spread over all the face of the earth" (*Bereishis* 41:56), that the phrase "the face of the earth" refers to the wealthy. The wealthy are referred to as the face of the earth since they are not embarrassed when dealing with people and they have no need to hide their faces. They have self-confidence.

It is important for a person to develop self-respect for himself and to build his own character. Although, of course, a person's intrinsic value has nothing to do with wealth, for many people, basic financial health does play a role in self-perception. Financial self-sufficiency can help a person develop his self-worth.

Flattery

"Those who forsake the Torah praise the wicked." (Mishlei 28:4)

The use of insincere compliments may be considered distasteful in contemporary society, but the Bible and the Sages considered it a serious character blemish, going so far as to deem it an outright sin.[7] The prophet Yeshayah says, "Sinners were afraid in Zion, trembling seized the flatterers" (33:14), *Mishlei* says, "with a flattering mouth one corrupts his friend..." (11:9), and the Sages also stated that the people were subject to Divine punishment for flattering King Agrippa.[8]

The Sages perceived flattery as a serious offense and character defect because it represents a type of "service" to people. At its core, it entails an element of denying G-d by trying to gain favors from people; it is as if the flatterer feels another person should provide for his needs. In a certain sense, flattery is worse than idolatry: While an idolater usually has a limited number of gods, the flatterer has an unlimited number of people whom he can flatter![9]

Financial self-sufficiency removes the need to flatter others.

Along these lines, the Sages state that one of the groups of people that cannot greet the Divine Presence is the "group of flatterers."[10] Because flatterers serve people, which is a form of rebellion against G-d, G-d reciprocates by not making His Divine Presence available to them, as it says, "The flatterer does not come before Him."[11]

In the area of finances, flattery is particularly relevant to those in need. The poor often resort to flattery to gain the favors they require to improve their situation. Financial self-sufficiency, on the other hand, removes the need to flatter others.[12]

It is interesting that both the wealthy and the poor run the risk of degrading their personality to the point that they border on "denial" of G-d, albeit from different angles. The person with vast amounts of wealth will forget that G-d has assisted him in his material success, while the poor man, through his subservience and fear of others, also

Both rich and poor run the risk of denying G-d in their beliefs around money.

denies G-d's omnipotence. Essentially, both men trust in wealth instead of G-d. The wealthy person sins if he trusts in his wealth, while the poor man sins if he believes that wealth will solve his problems. Thus, "A rich man's wealth is his citadel of strength, but poverty is the ruin of the impoverished."[13] Each looks at money from a different angle but both have reached a point where their beliefs around money have been corrupted and they have made almost the same mistake.

Poverty as a Cure

"The Holy One looked at all of the good attributes to give to Israel and the only good attribute He found for them was poverty. As people say, 'Poverty is fitting for Israel.'" (Chagigah 9b)

This aphorism of the Sages is difficult to understand. Why and in what way is poverty "fitting" for Israel? Does not the Torah itself promise great blessings of material bounty if the Children of Israel live their lives in accordance with its precepts?[14] Surely, then, wealth is fitting for Israel! Moreover, as seen earlier the Talmud itself states that suffering plagues is preferable to poverty.[15] How, then, could it be desirable?

Obviously, wealth is a blessing that makes man's life easier; it even assists in his service of G-d. Nevertheless, wealth is inherently dangerous, as it can ultimately corrupt a person's moral character and that of an entire nation. When the "spiritual diseases" of haughtiness, brazenness, and lack of trust in G-d set in, the Almighty has a powerful weapon to help correct the ways of man: poverty. Poverty is thus fitting for Israel because it is the cure for the maladies induced by wealth. Indeed, historically, the Jewish nation has flourished under conditions of poverty, whereas the blessing of wealth has not always been conducive to success in maintaining its eternal mission.[16]

If, however, a person is impoverished to the point at which he is unable to provide for his family's needs, then on all accounts it is undesirable. In fact, the *Medrash* says that the affliction of poverty is so insidious that it can be compared to all other sufferings put together.[17] This level of poverty is not necessary to cure the diseases of wealth.[18] The Sages therefore teach people to pray that they should not be subjected to this extreme level of poverty.[19]

Furthermore, while poverty may be G-d's tool for healing the nation, it does not mean that people should actively pursue it. Man is obligated to provide for his needs and the needs of his family, which necessitates trying to stay *out of* poverty. In fact, the Sages instruct people to avoid poverty.[20] The success of a person's endeavors is in G-d's hands; it is He who determines whether an individual or community will be impoverished. It is the individual's responsibility, however, to put in the effort.

> *Man is required to exert himself to avoid poverty. His success is in the hands of G-d.*

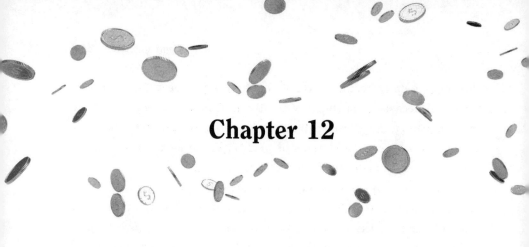

Chapter 12

Wealth

It is also crucial to understand the purpose of wealth and its role in the life of man. How does a person's wealth impact who he is? How is wealth valued and perceived? Man exists in a material world and it is easy to get caught up in the hustle-bustle and lose sight of the Torah's perspective on these issues.

The Purpose of Wealth

"The acts of the righteous are for life." (Mishlei 10:16)

A *tzaddik* knows better than to rely on his wealth or to be concerned with his lack of it. When it comes to the resources that are available to a *tzaddik*, his entire goal is to use his assets to serve G-d and to advance His honor; he works for a living in order to attain the ability to dedicate time to serving G-d through study and contemplation. In addition, he uses his wealth to support others who seek to serve G-d. All of these intentions are "for life." Serving G-d in all endeavors, including the utilization of wealth, is life-giving.[1]

Rambam writes that the Sages encapsulated one of the most important concepts in the entire Torah in one short phrase: "All your actions should be for the sake of Heaven."[2]

Man has the ability to elevate all aspects of his life, even the most mundane, by acting for the sake of Heaven. If he eats and sleeps with

114

the purpose of giving his body the strength to serve G-d, then those actions become quasi-mitzvos. Thus, Rambam writes:

> When one is involved with acquiring wealth, one's intent should be for the purpose of using it for elevated matters. In addition, it should be used for maintaining one's physical existence in order that he should be able to acquire knowledge of G-d according to his ability.[3]

The pursuit of wealth is uplifted with the appropriate intentions. If the goal of acquiring wealth is to help one perform mitzvos or to enable a person to pursue knowledge of G-d, then these endeavors become "acts for the sake of Heaven," even while the person is involved in worldly matters.

Buying Eternity

"Hear this all you nations; give ear, all you inhabitants of the fleeting world." (Tehillim 49:2)

When the psalmist seeks to teach about the relationship between man's material possessions and his moral and spiritual task in life, he calls out to all of mankind to hear his words. This is not a particularly Jewish issue, but rather one pertinent to all of humanity. The psalmist teaches that only by a person fulfilling his purpose on earth — and employing his physical and material resources as a means to that end — can man rescue his spiritual existence so that it will reach beyond his fleeting time on earth. If man fails to recognize his true purpose and instead views the acquisition of wealth as an end in and of itself, he will forfeit immortality and his existence will not continue beyond the grave.[4]

Thus, the Sages said, "Gold was only created to be used in the Sanctuary."[5] Wealth is supposed to be a means for man to fulfill his duties to G-d, including supporting himself, performing mitzvos, and doing charitable acts. Indeed, the *Chovos HaLevavos* writes that one of the reasons man must work for a living is so that he may observe the relevant commandments and merit the next world.[6] When a person recognizes this, his wealth becomes a means of achieving eternity, of redeeming his Divine soul. On the other hand, if he fails to use his possessions properly, the psalmist says, "And it [the soul] shall cease to be forever" (*Tehillim* 49:9).[7]

Plaques

"Yosef, son of Yoezer, donated a roomful of silver coins and his son donated six rooms." (Bava Basra 133b)

When used properly, not only can wealth be used to merit eternity by using it for worthy causes, but its merit can be magnified when it serves as a source of inspiration for others as well.

The Talmud relates that Yosef, son of Yoezer, cut off his son's inheritance because of the son's improper conduct. Instead of allowing his wealth to transfer to his son, he made a large donation to the Temple. The son took this to heart and eventually changed his ways. When he came to possess a rare stone that could be used in the breastplate of the High Priest, he donated a large portion of the value of this stone to the Temple, thereby surpassing the donation of his father. The Sages recorded this great donation in a special book in which great deeds were recorded so that future generations could remember them.

The idea of recording great deeds for posterity is found in the Torah and was the practice of the prophets as well.[8] This is the source for the practice of placing plaques in synagogues, study halls, and other institutions to recognize those who made them possible. In this way, by using wealth to support holy activities not only can a person make a direct impact on those receiving the donation, but he can also serve as an inspiration to others. Thus, it is appropriate to record and honor people who use their wealth to support G-d's causes.

Paying tribute to those who use their wealth to honor G-d will inspire others.

Values and Value

"Silver was not considered to be of any worth in the days of Shlomo." (*Divrei HaYamim II 9:20*)

In the time of Shlomo, gold was in such abundance that even the king's drinking cups were made of gold. The abundance of gold reduced the value of silver to such a point that it says, "silver was not worth anything."[9] Yet, elsewhere, *Sefer Melachim* says that Shlomo Hamelech made "silver as common as stones," indicating that silver did have some value, albeit limited.[10] The Talmud reconciles the contradictory verses by suggesting that one verse refers to the period before Shlomo married the daughter of Pharaoh, whereas the other verse describes the time after they married.[11] Only after this marriage did silver take on "value."

What does this marriage have to do with the value of silver?

Silver is valuable as a precious metal that can be used in commerce, and it has many industrial applications as well. Aside from its economic value, which can be measured against other metals, currencies or objects, there is another subtler aspect when discussing the value of silver (money). This is its value when measured against other values. In other words, how does silver (money) rate alongside other values such as life, wisdom, education, etc.? It is in this area of value that there was a change from the period prior to Shlomo Hamelech's marriage to the daughter of Pharaoh and afterward. Ultimately, this change in values was reflected by a change in its monetary value. What happened? What did this marriage represent?

According to the Talmud, the marriage of Shlomo Hamelech to the daughter of Pharaoh was one of the great tragedies of Jewish history, as it sowed the seeds for the destruction of the First Temple. It was at that point that a major change took place in Jewish society: The value of wisdom, in particular Torah wisdom, decreased ever so slightly in

Subtle perceptions and attitudes toward money can have a noticeable effect on people and society.

the eyes of the people. At the same time, the importance of worldly pleasure increased, as reflected in the growing significance of silver. The moral fabric of society began to weaken with seemingly small changes in attitude, ultimately paving the way for complete destruction.[12]

Perceptions around wealth and money reflect the values of society at large. These values have a major impact on individuals as well as on the entire community.

Inherent Value

"So says the L-rd: Let not the wise man glory in his wisdom, and let not the strong man glory in his strength; let not the rich man glory in his wealth. For in this shall the one who glorifies himself glorify — comprehending and knowing Me." (Yirmeyah 9:22–23)

Yirmeyah mentions three traits that people should not praise themselves for: wisdom, strength, and wealth. Of all three, it would seem most appropriate for man to glorify in his wisdom, as this is part of a person's essence, setting man apart from the rest of creation. Nevertheless, Yirmeyah says that a person should not take pride even in this achievement, let alone in the acquisition of wealth. Indeed, while wisdom and strength are gifts from G-d, they are not attained without some effort on man's part. Wealth, on the other hand, can come to a person without any effort at all, as is the case with an inheritance or winning a lottery.

Humans generally honor wealth more than wisdom; however, by placing wealth last in the verse, Yirmeyah teaches that since wealth is entirely dependent on the will of G-d and remains completely external to the person, it is

> *Of all of man's achievements, wealth is the least worthy of praise. However, praising those that use it to serve G-d is proper.*

the least deserving of praise.[13] Only knowing G-d — imitating and following His ways — is worthy of honor.[14]

Moreover, wealth is essentially valueless. As discussed before, its purpose is to serve as a means to attain higher goals and, ultimately, to merit the next world. In the next world — man's ultimate destination — monetary wealth is of no value; money has no function once man is the grave. Thus, at its most basic level, there is no difference between gold and the dirt of the earth.[15] If people understood the lack of inherent value in wealth, they would recognize the folly in honoring it.

Failure to Understand

"The heart of man is full of evil." (*Koheles 9:3*)

All people, even those devoted to spiritual pursuits, must take some time to care for their physical needs. This, inevitably, requires some form of involvement with money and commerce. Since all people are involved in these activities, it is easy to conclude that the pursuit of livelihood is a purpose unto itself and perhaps even one of man's primary purposes in the world. Shlomo Hamelech bemoaned this error when he described the heart of man as "evil." His point was that man fails to realize his purpose in fulfilling temporary, physical needs, and this leads him astray.[16]

In a similar vein, a person can observe the righteous engaged in business or a trade and conclude that he should follow a similar pursuit. The problem is that most people see only the external actions but fail to see what goes on inside the other person's mind. The righteous go out to earn their livelihood with specific purposes. All of their actions embody the service of G-d; their intent is in all

It is often necessary to see beyond one's own eyes to understand reality.

that they do. Consequently, their pursuit of a livelihood becomes a service of G-d, while for others who do not understand this, it is more likely to become a pursuit without purpose. Their failure to see beyond their own eyes misleads them.[17]

In this world, it is often difficult to discern what is truly good. Only through the regular study of the Sage's words can people gain clarity and remove the evil to which Shlomo Hamelech refers.

Mistaken Identity

"G-d will not let the soul of the righteous hunger, and the money of the evil man He will push away." (Mishlei 10:3)

The Hebrew word used as a reference to money in the verse above is *havas*. This word has a number of meanings. It can be translated as money or wealth so that the meaning of this verse (as translated above) is that G-d will push the money of the evil man away.[18]

The word *havas* can also be related to the word *hoveh* which translates as "being" or "existing." With this meaning, the verse can be understood to refer to a specific type of evil person — one who believes his identity is intertwined with his wealth. Thus, G-d will push his existence away. By taking his money, G-d is taking his existence, as they are one and the same in his eyes: This is his essence. This misconception will ultimately lead to his downfall in a measure-for-measure type of punishment. G-d's response is to bring him to a state in which he is separated from his wealth, he will then realize his folly!

Havas also means "destruction." This is, indeed, is its more common usage, and it adds an additional nuance to the verse. Accordingly, it teaches that when a person views wealth as part of his very essence, the wealth itself will lead to his destruction and its loss. Similarly, Shlomo Hamelech wrote that "riches hoarded by their owner to his misfortune."[19] Wealth can harm its owners if they view it as the purpose of their existence.

> *A person should never let wealth become part of his core identity.*

In contrast, the first portion of the verse, "G-d will not let the soul of the righteous man hunger," teaches that the reverse is true for the righteous. A righteous person recognizes that his wealth is not part of his essence; it is a gift from G-d to be managed with good stewardship. It is not to be acquired through ill-gotten means or by withholding it from those in need. Thus, he is willing to give to the poor and others who are in need of monetary contributions. While it may appear that this will decrease a person's net worth, G-d will replenish it.[20]

Dependents

*"As goods increase, so do those who consume them; what
advantage, then has the owner except what his eyes see?
The satiety of the rich does not let him sleep."* (Koheles 5:9–11)

It is crucial for a person to understand why he is pursuing wealth.
Some pursue wealth so they can live a life of luxury. A lifestyle of
opulence often entails increasing the number of people dependent
upon the wealthy person, such as servants or employees. The wealthy
person may even take pleasure in seeing his staff grow. This is part of
enjoying his wealth. His employees need him and he is "on top;" he
has a mini-empire. This man of means then becomes obligated (or at
least feels obligated) to retain their support, which drives him to work
more and more in order to sustain those who are dependent upon him.
Koheles concludes that these increased obligations actually have no benefit. They do not help the rich man achieve perfection of character, and
his wealth will not be of any benefit in the next world. His increase in
wealth brings with it only unnecessary worry and concern.[21] It is preferable for a person to be satisfied with taking care of his needs and not
look for a life of luxury that will obligate him to work to support others.

This concept is also alluded to in the words of the Sages, "Who is
wealthy? One who is happy with his portion."[22] His portion is what is
necessary for him and his immediate family, not for those outside of
this unit. A person who must work to support others is not included
among the wealthy, as his circumstances are actually negative."[23]
Abarbanel suggests a proof to this concept: the Sages support their own
statement from *Tehillim*, "When you eat of the work of your labor, you
are wealthy and it is good for you,"[24] which underscores the statement
in the *mishnah* that a wealthy man is one who is happy with his portion.
It is a great achievement and blessing from G-d when through the work
of his hands a man can provide for himself, his wife, and his children,
who are enumerated in the next verse, "Your wife will be like a fruitful
vine in the inner chambers of your home and your children will be like

olive shoots surrounding your table." Since it mentions a wife and children, the psalm teaches that the parameters of "his portion" include the nuclear family. Working for those outside his family is excessive and is considered going beyond working for "his portion."

Koheles teaches that it is of no advantage to increase wealth for the benefit of dependents, but this has nothing to do with charitable donations. Just as a man takes care of his family, he should also help those who are in need. This is not a luxury, but a basic obligation. *Koheles* is teaching people to pursue self-support and not look for a life of luxury that will bring with it an increased number of dependents.

> *The Sages emphasized that a person should work to support his family, not to seek a life of luxury.*

Today, dependents do not take the form of servants and slaves, but of objects. Additional homes, cars, boats, and the like, all increase a person's overhead and require him to find the means to maintain them. Consequently, the owner is required to work even more to support all of his possessions. This is what is meant by, "The satiety of the rich does not let him sleep."

Danger to Character

"And you may say in your heart, 'My strength and the might of my hand made me all of this wealth!'" (Devarim 8:17)

The primary concern the Sages had regarding wealth was that a person would come to lose sight of G-d's role in his success. This idea is expressed in the Torah itself: "Yeshurun became fat and kicked" (*Devarim* 32:15). Monetary success brings with it an inherent danger. When man is successful in his endeavors, it seems like it was his "genius" that led to his prosperity, when in reality it was G-d who enabled him to succeed. Failing to see G-d's role is akin to denying G-d's omnipotence, which is a fundamental Jewish belief. Ultimately, success can lead to outright denial of G-d: "Lest I be sated and deny You."[25]

Haughtiness is one of the major character flaws that wealth can foster. This trait is held in disdain by the Torah: "Every haughty heart is the abomination of G-d" (*Mishlei* 16:5).[26] Since wealth is one major cause of this key character defect, the Sages were concerned with the inherent dangers of excessive wealth. Indeed, the Torah outlines the trajectory of wealth, haughtiness, and ultimate denial of G-d: "And you increase gold and silver for yourselves and all your possessions will increase and your heart will become haughty and you will forget G-d" (*Devarim* 8:13–14).

Another character defect fostered by wealth is brazenness: "And the wealthy answer with brazenness" (*Mishlei* 18:23). In addition to leading to sin, being brazen is in and of itself a sin.[27] The Torah relates that the reason that G-d chose to reveal Himself to the entire nation at Mount Sinai was so that the "awe of G-d would be on their faces."[28] The Talmud explains that this awesome event led to the quality of *boshes panim* (bashfulness), which ultimately leads to proper fear of G-d.[29] It follows that the purpose of this awesome event was to foster the trait of *boshes panim* in the entire nation. Clearly, then, the opposite trait, *azus panim* (insolence), must be avoided as much as possible.[30] The *mishnah* teaches, "a brazen person goes to Gehinnom and a bashful person will merit the Garden of Eden."[31] Brazenness leads to rejecting those who can guide others on the appropriate path, thereby putting a person on course for Gehinnom.[32]

> *Haughtiness and brazenness are two areas in which the wealthy must be careful.*

Brazenness can also push a person to the point at which he cannot tolerate those who disagree with him: "A rich man is wise in his own eyes" (*Mishlei* 28:11). When he is engaged is some form of debate, he will persist and do anything to ensure that his position wins the day, even if it entails resorting to false stratagems and lies. His wealth brings him to the point that he is no longer interested in truth — only in success.[33]

Finally, people often refrain from correcting or criticizing a wealthy person, even when he is acting improperly. As a result, he does not receive any guidance and may continue to act improperly. Moreover, he serves as a poor role model for others who try to emulate those who are successful. If the wealthy man has strayed from the proper path, others may follow in the ways of his folly. Not only is he on a path of self-destruction, he brings others along for the ride.

If a person is aware of these concerns, then with vigilance and the proper course of study, he can prevent wealth from damaging his character. It is only when he neglects personal growth and character refinement that he is in danger. On the other hand, sensitivity to this problem can enable a person to overcome the dangers of wealth and allow him to flourish. For this reason, the Sages do not renounce wealth entirely; they simply caution against its dangers. Avraham, Yitzchak, and Yaakov were all wealthy

> *Sensitivity to the challenges of wealth can enable its owner to achieve great heights.*

and serve as paradigms of how to serve G-d in every aspect of life. Rabbi Yehuda HaNasi, the redactor and editor of the Mishnah, also had great wealth and yet was one of the great examples of humility and separation from worldly pleasures — to the point that he is known as own as Rabbeinu HaKodesh (the holy teacher).[34] There is no inherent problem in wealth. It only becomes a "problem" when the person does not understand how to relate to it.

All Being Equal

"Better a pauper who walks in his innocence than one who perverts his lips and is a fool." (Mishlei 19:1)

As seen earlier, both poverty and wealth can impact a person's character in an adverse manner. However, there is a crucial difference between the two.

Poverty causes a person to be in need of others and is therefore a blemish on the person; but as long as he does not flatter the wealthy, his character is not flawed due to his deprivation. On the other hand, a rich person who speaks brazenly because of his wealth has a character defect so significant that this alone makes him a fool.[35]

Rabbeinu Eliyahu of Vilna, better known as the Vilna Gaon (1720–1797), writes that it is man's purpose in this world to continually perfect himself.[36] If wealth is going to lead to defects in character, then poverty is preferable, even with its negative consequences. People must take care to ensure that their financial situation is not detrimental to their character.[37]

Advantages of Wealth

"The crown of the wise is their wealth." (Mishlei 14:24)

Despite the fact that wealth from a purely spiritual view point is without value and carries with it many negative facets, the Sages speak about many advantages of wealth. From their perspective, these advantages have nothing to do with the ability to afford fine homes, cars, and clothing, but with how wealth can be used for good.

Wealth serves as a companion to wisdom, completing the picture or adding a "crown." A wise man may not be honored properly if he lacks monetary wealth; people might feel he does not deserve honor. In contrast, if he has wealth then he will receive the honor that is rightfully his. More importantly, when a Torah scholar has monetary means, his words are more readily accepted since people may not give credence to the words of a poor scholar, as it says, "a poor man's wisdom is despised" (*Koheles* 9:16). Thus, when wealth is paired with wisdom, the scholar is able to spread Torah and truth, enabling him to implement his wisdom in this world.

Another role that a scholar may play is to work against the wicked and other forces of evil. Often, it takes monetary resources to implement the teachings of the Torah. When a scholar has wealth, he is positioned to use his own funds to support and enhance these causes. In doing so, he makes wealth his crowning glory. Wealth remains, however, a "crown." It is not part of the scholar's essence, but it simply "sits" on him. Just as a crown enhances the one who wears it, wealth enhances the stature of the scholar.[38]

Wealth enhances the role of the scholar.

Priorities

"Pens for the flocks we will build here for the livestock and cities for our small children." (Bamidbar 32:16)

The tribes of Gad and Reuven did not want to cross over the Jordan River to inherit their portions in the Land of Israel. Instead, they wished to remain on the eastern bank of the Jordan, as this region was more suitable for their sheep and cattle. In their request to Moshe, they said that they wished to build pens for their flocks and homes for their children, putting their property before their family. In his response, Moshe

The proper attitude toward wealth is paramount to enjoy its full benefit.

reversed the order: "Build for yourselves cities for your small children and pens for your flock" (Bamidbar 32:24). He thus indicated that their priorities had become confused.

While wealth is certainly useful and has numerous benefits, the proper attitude toward it is crucial. The Sages comment that when wealth is valued above things of true value such as family, it will ultimately lack blessing.[39] The blessing that wealth provides depends upon a person's attitude toward it.

The Wisdom to Use Wealth Properly

"You bestow man with understanding." (Daily Amidah Prayer)

In composing the *Amidah*, the silent prayer made up of eighteen blessings, the *Anshei K'nesses HaGedolah* included numerous requests for fulfillment of basic needs, such as sustenance and health. The first request is for wisdom. By placing this request first, the Sages teach that the value of man's worldly needs must be preceded by wisdom. Man requires wisdom to pursue and achieve even his basic needs. Furthermore, the blessings that man seeks from G-d are complete only when coupled with the wisdom to use the fruits of his efforts properly. Wisdom enables true success by providing the insight in how to use that which G-d provides man. The Sages put the blessing of wisdom first because it is the foundation of all that follows.[40]

Thus, in the daily prayers, as it relates to wealth, the Sages instituted that people ask G-d to bestow various forms of understanding and intelligence so they

Prayer is necessary to help recognize and appreciate the value and purpose of wealth.

can appreciate and recognize the value and meaning of wealth, including the understanding and perspective to properly utilize that which G-d provides them — the fruits of their labor.

Chapter 13

Needs and Wants

The world abounds with opportunities to enjoy and experience its physical and material bounty; however, much of this abundance comes with a price. Enjoyment of the physical world often comes at the expense of the spiritual world. While man is obligated to provide and care for his physical needs, when he takes too much, it becomes detrimental to his spiritual life.

The key question a person must ask when engaging in physical pleasure or acquiring things is whether those pleasures or possessions are needed or only desired. The distinction between needs and wants plays an important role in the Sages' outlook on wealth. It is, in fact, part of their litmus test to determine who is wealthy. Understanding the difference between the two is essential, regardless of how much money a person has. Even the very wealthy, who can satisfy all of their heart's desires, need to understand the difference. The availability of something does not necessarily mean it is wise to partake of it. As always, the Sages are guided by their concern for spiritual well-being when approaching physical pleasures. While some wants are certainly permissible, recognizing the difference between needs and wants is one of the most fundamental elements of relating to wealth.

Who Is Wealthy?

"Who is wealthy? One who is happy with his portion." (Avos 4:1)

According to the Sages, wealth reflects a person's state of mind, not the state of his bank accounts. A person is wealthy when he is satisfied with what he has — when he is not absorbed in the desire for more material possessions, not necessarily when he has the greatest net worth. In contrast, a person who always feels that he needs more is considered poor, even if he has amassed vast amounts of money. When a person feels he is lacking, he is essentially impoverished.

Wealth, when evaluated in terms of satisfaction with what a person has, reflects on man's overall happiness. *Mishlei* states, "All the days of a poor man are bad, but a good-hearted person feasts perpetually."[1] When someone is "poor," he is not satisfied with his own portion but rather he desires the wealth of others, and he will never be satisfied; he is thus condemned to unhappiness. A person who is happy with his portion — a person who possesses the trait of *histapkus* (satisfaction) — will always be happy, regardless of his financial state.[2]

There is, however, an important caveat in this context. Rabbeinu Yonah describes the wealthy person as one who says: "What I have is sufficient for me, since I am able to support myself and family and to study Torah. Why do I need more money as long as I have what I need and can perform G-d's commandments?"[3] A person must pursue his needs. He should be happy with what he has under the condition that it supports his

Wealth according to the Sages is a state of mind; however, it does require that basic needs be satisfied.

needs and enables him to learn Torah and perform mitzvos. If he does not have enough money to take care of himself and his family, it is inappropriate to say, "What do I need with additional money?" Such a person is not "wealthy," even if he declares that he is happy with his lot. While wealth is a state of mind, it also requires that basic needs be met.[4]

Satisfaction

"...if so much as a thread to a shoe strap; or if I will take from anything that is yours." (Bereishis 14:23)

The Sages refer to one of Avraham's outstanding qualities as *ayin tovah*.[5] One who has a good eye is satisfied with what he has; he is not interested in luxuries.[6] Because his life does not revolve around worldly pleasures, he does not desire more than he needs.[7] In contrast, someone with an *ayin ra'ah* is always jealous of others and always scheming to obtain what others have. He is never satisfied, even when his needs are met. Having mastered the trait of *ayin tovah*, Avraham refused to take his share in the booty from a war that he himself had won. Content with his lot, he saw no need to take even the smallest of items from the spoils.[8]

Avraham embodied the quality of satisfaction, and the Sages maintain that it is one of the three essential traits exhibited by the "students of Avraham."[9] The quality of satisfaction is further reflected in the prohibition of coveting, the last of the Ten Commandments, which represents an entire category of commandments geared toward limiting desire for worldly possessions.[10] A follower of Avraham does not constantly look over his shoulder at what his neighbor has because he is satisfied with his own portion.

The followers of Avraham are satisfied with their portion and do not feel they are lacking anything.

On the opposite extreme is Bilaam,[11] whose desire for wealth was boundless. Indeed, his insatiable desire for wealth was one of the foremost aspects of his wickedness. Balak, king of Moav, hired Bilaam to place a curse on the Children of Israel in exchange for great wealth. Bilaam accepted the offer even though he knew he could not transgress the will of G-d to accomplish his task. Upon setting out on his journey, he was aware that G-d did not want him to go, but he continued nonetheless. The possibility of obtaining a great fortune drove him to make the effort, but ultimately, his desire for wealth resulted in the death of thousands of people, including himself.

The Middle Road

"What is the proper path that a person should choose for himself?" (Avos 2:1)

Rambam writes that the middle path is appropriate in nearly all of a person's *de'os* (attitudes) and character traits.[12] The middle path is similarly recommended when it comes to the attitude toward wealth. At one extreme, a person's desires for physical pleasure and wealth are so great that they completely dominate his being. In the language of the Sages, such a person is referred to as being a *ba'al nefesh rechavah*, literally a person with a broad soul, and *nivhal lehon*, one who is overeager for wealth.[13] Extremes in the realm of attitudes lead to extremes in action; a person who cannot satiate his desire for wealth will do nearly anything he can to achieve it. On the other end of the spectrum is a person who is lazy and therefore does not work at all. While his desires are not out of control, he fails to provide even for his basic needs, which is also not the Torah's desire.

A person must seek the middle road with respect to the de'ah of wealth. This is known as histapkus, satisfaction.

The "middle road" approach to wealth is referred to as *ayin tovah*, which Rambam defines as *histapkus*. In other words, the middle path is where a person is satisfied with his needs being met and does not desire more. A person who is satisfied with what he has will work enough to provide for his needs, and he will then be able to devote himself to Torah. He realizes that too much work will take away from his Torah studies, while no work will leave him without support.[14]

The Divine Command

"In all your ways know Him." (Mishlei 3:6)

While a person might understand the Sages' instruction to be satisfied with his portion as simply good advice and appropriate guidance for those who wish to achieve great levels of piety, Rabbeinu Bachya ibn Paquda explains that this is an incorrect analysis of the Sages' teachings. Satisfaction with the fulfillment of basic needs and overcoming the desire to accumulate greater material wealth is an essential part of the fulfillment of G-d's commandments, not a goal for the especially righteous. Ultimately, Rabbeinu Bachya writes, everything in this world falls under the rubric of a Divine command. The Torah has positive and negative commandments governing an enormous range of human activity, nonetheless, a large span of life remains outside this formal framework of rules and regulations. Still, Rabbeinu Bachya states that even these matters which are left to individual choice are governed by the command of G-d.[15] *Koheles* teaches, "For G-d will judge every deed, even everything hidden, whether good or evil."[16] All of man's activities are within the framework of the Divine command. As such, when people pursue material goods beyond their needs, it is not simply a lack of piety — it is a violation of a negative precept. When people pursue their needs, in contrast, they fulfill a Divine precept.[17]

For example, once the dietary laws have been observed, the question of what and how much to eat is a matter of free choice: A person can eat more than he needs, precisely what he needs, or even less than he needs. When he chooses more or less than he needs, he may be in violation of this general command to seek his needs. It would depend upon his intent. Consequently, everything a person does falls under the command of G-d.[18] G-d does not want physical desires to rule over man. When desire takes hold of man and he seeks more than he needs, the experience becomes sinful. Along these lines Rambam writes that a person must

G-d's commandments encompass all aspects of life.

repent for "the pursuit of food."[19] To desire more than a person needs is to violate a Divine precept.[20] Therefore, according to this approach, it is crucial that a person determine what his needs truly are, as even his mundane choices must reflect the Divine will. Intent in the pursuit of wealth will determine whether his efforts constitute the fulfillment of G-d's command or the violation thereof.

Needs and Wants

*"…and give to me bread to eat
and clothing to wear." (Bereishis 28:20)*

It is essential to differentiate between what is a "need" and what is a "want"; however, making this determination can often be challenging. While the Sages are clear that a person should seek to fill his needs, they did not provide clear guidelines as to what is a need and what is not. Undoubtedly, in many situations the distinction between the two is clear, but there remains a large gray area which a person must discern for himself. There are many factors that should be considered when making this evaluation. Even for one person there are things which at one time might be luxuries and at other times necessities (see section on "Spending for Happiness"). What is clear is that needs and wants depend on an individual's unique situation.

When Yaakov fled from his brother Esav, he prayed to G-d to provide him with clothing and food. These are some of the most basic human needs. At that point in time, as a single man, this was all he needed. Yaakov modeled being satisfied with the most essential needs. In fact, this is the most basic definition of needs, things that are necessary to function. Even this will vary from place to place and in different historical periods. Nonetheless, *Chovos HaLevavos* states that with respect to one's bodily needs, such as food, there is a guarantee that G-d will provide for it.[21]

Once a person is married, his needs change. The Talmud, when discussing whether a person should study prior to marriage or marry and study afterward, exclaims, "A millstone around his neck and he should learn Torah?"[22] It is clear from this that since he is married, his needs and his obligations are different, and this will impact on his studies and other aspects of his life. The addition of children will increase a person's needs even further. This is clear from Yaakov who — after building his family while working for his father-in-law — says, "And now when will I also do something for my own house?"[23] Yaakov was aware that his circumstances had changed and that he had an obligation to provide for his family.[24] Even if his own personal needs had not changed and he could still live with very little, his obligations had changed and this required him to seek more than he had in the past. A man has an obligation to his wife and children which, in the end, changes his needs. Taken further, a king has even greater responsibilities to his people, so his needs are even greater, and yet although he requires great resources to sustain his kingdom, it still is viewed as a need. Kings simply require more than other people.

Chovos HaLevavos makes an interesting distinction between a person's personal needs and those of his family. He writes there is no guarantee for all men that the needs of his family will be met, although G-d does provide this out of righteousness and kindliness.[25] Apparently, the guarantee to man is only on personal needs, not personal obligations.

Unfortunately, even understanding these principles will not provide clarity in determining needs and wants. This will require analysis. For example, if a person needs a car because he has to get from here to there, it is a need. There are many types and models of cars available, all of which should be able to provide for his needs; some will provide much more than just his needs. Of course there are other factors that impact on this decision, such as financing, quality, service, warranty, etc. Still at some point the individual will have to choose and this will require that he be honest with himself as to why he is choosing a specific model. Is his choice driven by wants and desires for things that the car offers that he does not really need? This question can be applied in all areas, even to that which is essential. Clothing is an essential need, but there is room to question whether a $1,000 suit is necessary. The same concept holds true for children. Summer camp can be viewed as indispensable for a child, and parents need to provide for this necessity. The question of which camp or program should be selected, however, may become a question of needs and wants. It will depend on the individual situation.

In short, in order to determine whether something is a "need" or "want," a person needs to focus on why he wants a particular thing and what its purpose is in his life. Needs can go beyond that which is absolutely necessary for survival and can include obligations one has toward others, such as a wife and children.

There is another type of need as well. There are many things that people do not need to survive, but to help their overall emotional well-being. These are things that help maintain overall happiness and good mental health. For example, a home to live in is essential. What about decorations for the home? These also can be essential, since for most people it is depressing to live in a bare space. Still, when it comes to choosing the specific decorations a person will have to make an assessment about each particular item. Is it beyond what is needed? In each situation, the individual must make an honest assessment about his needs.

Since determining needs and wants ultimately requires an honest evaluation by the person given his set of circumstances, it can be helpful to study the words of the Sages regularly and to review their emphasis regarding taking care of needs and avoiding extras. Although they will not be discussing a contemporary situation, their words will often help the searching soul find what it is looking for.

Life of Simplicity

"One should not accustom his children to meat and wine." (Chulin 84a)

Scripture and the Sages repeatedly stress the importance of satisfaction with essentials and avoidance of pursuing luxury. Shlomo

Hamelech tells us, "Let the lambs be your clothing...and let the milk of goats be sufficient for your food, and the food of your household, and give life to your maidens" (*Mishlei* 27:26–27). Goats and sheep should not be used as sources of meat, but rather as sources of wool and milk. The optimal lifestyle entails modest — not luxurious — clothing and food. Even Shlomo Hamelech, who was extremely wealthy, preaches that one should not desire luxuries.[26]

By teaching his family to be satisfied with a modest lifestyle, freeing them of the need to obtain more and more, a man provides them with a vital lesson for life, thus the phrase, "and life to your maidens." Teaching this approach provides "life" to a person's children as it provides for them an approach that will serve them well throughout their lifetime. The best time to inculcate these values is when children are young.

> *A person should train his children to live a modest lifestyle.*

Indeed, this is part of the moral education that a man must provide to prepare his children for life as adults. And, even if a person is not raised that way, he should train himself to live modestly.[27]

Desires beyond One's Needs

"For his mouth presses upon him." (*Mishlei* 16:26)

The pursuit of excessive pleasure has other negative consequences as well. A person who constantly seeks to fulfill his desires ultimately ends up wasting his life away in the service of his physical "needs," rather than in the service of G-d. Rabbeinu Yonah explains that "for his mouth presses upon him" means "the needs of his mouth weigh him down."[28] His pursuit of gastronomic pleasure requires that he spend more time in the pursuit of money. Gastronomic pleasures are symbolic of a lifestyle of luxury. The person does not see anything wrong in a lavish way of life since he does not violate any formal prohibitions. Yet, over time he will be involved with frivolous pursuits and fail to care properly for his soul. Thus, Rabbeinu Yonah interprets the beginning of the verse above, "the soul works for the worker," to mean that the soul works for the body, which is the opposite of what should be: when the body works for the soul.

When a person is dominated by physical desires, he is left with little time for his soul. The planning necessary for his pursuits takes a great deal of time and effort, and he becomes obsessed with his elusive goal of attaining greater wealth. Even if he ultimately succeeds in attaining one goal, he will then turn his attention to other desires. Building a home, obtaining possessions, traveling, planning parties...they all consume time, energy, and resources, and when one project is finished, the cycle inevitably begins again.

In the long term, pursuit of excessive wealth and satisfaction of desires is a subtle path toward self-destruction. The more time and focus spent on this world and its pleasures ultimately weakens a person's connection with G-d, and the more disconnected he becomes from spiritual matters, the more difficult it becomes to reconnect to them.[29] It is obviously necessary to partake in the physical world, but a person's

> *Desires that are out of control will result in the soul serving the body, the opposite of what was intended.*

desires must remain in check so that he has the time and energy to focus on what truly matters. In this vein Shlomo Hamelech teaches, "Desire broken is sweet to the soul" (*Mishlei* 13:19).

This perspective obligates serious introspection. A person should be asking himself: Why am I eating, and what am I eating? Why am I going to work? If a person determines that his desires are excessive, compelling him to spend more time taking care of his physical needs, he should take serious note. He may be on a path to ruin! By analyzing the most basic human activities, a person can

> *Healthy desires slowly growing beyond their needs might be a sign of spiritual decline.*

determine where he is putting his focus and whether it is in line with G-d's intent for man. Even when performing the mitzvos properly, if desires grow beyond what is necessary, the potential exists to destroy a person spiritually.[30]

A Waste of Time and Energy

"Do not weary yourself to become rich;
forbear from your own understanding." (Mishlei 23:4)

The sentence, "Do not weary yourself to become rich" teaches people not to waste energy in the pursuit of becoming wealthy once their needs have been satisfied. Once a person's needs have been satisfied, he can achieve the true definition of being wealthy — that of being satisfied with his portion. At that point, it is not necessary to pursue additional wealth. The next verse explains why: "For it [wealth] makes itself wings for itself, [and] like an eagle, it soars to the heavens."[31] Ultimately, material wealth is in G-d's hands: It comes and goes, sometimes "flying away" before man's very eyes. It is futile to spend energy in the pursuit of something that can so easily slip away! Pursuing wealth unnecessarily causes people to lose time and energy, precious and irreplaceable commodities that could have been used in the service of G-d.[32]

Another explanation as to why a person should not weary himself in

Man must use his energy wisely.

the pursuit of wealth is that if someone over-exerts himself in the pursuit of wealth, it will hinder him from acquiring wisdom; that is, it will "hold [you] back from your own understanding." How sad it is when that which should provide support for the pursuit of wisdom becomes the reason a person fails to acquire it.[33]

Enjoying This World

"I did not deprive myself of any kind of joy." (Koheles 2:10)

As previously mentioned, the Sages put great importance on people being satisfied with their portion, going so far as to define wealth in terms of satisfaction with one's lot. Yet, other statements of the Sages appear to contradict this idea. For example, they teach that:

> A person will have to give an accounting to the Master of the
> World for everything that he saw and did not wish to eat,

although he was permitted and able to do so...as the verse
states, "Anything my eyes asked, I did not keep from them."
(Koheles 2:10)³⁴

Here, it appears the Sages are teaching that people should make an attempt to enjoy everything the world has to offer. How can this be reconciled with the emphasis on being satisfied with the fulfillment of a person's basic needs?

One explanation is that whenever the Sages encouraged a person to benefit from this world, they were referring to that which is necessary. A person is permitted to enjoy this world and he should take from it what he needs. Danger lies in going beyond this point, and for that reason, the Sages encouraged a person to disconnect from the pursuit of unnecessary things.³⁵ Thus the accounting referred to here is whether the person enjoyed various foods in satisfying his needs. In no way did the Sages encourage taking any more than this. Satisfaction with needs being met is not only sufficient, but it is ideal.

Today, worldly pleasures are available more than ever before in the history of humanity. Food from all over the world is delivered to local supermarkets. Clothing, cars, electronics, and more arrive from all over the globe. All of this is available at prices that are within the means of most of the population. At the same time,

Satisfaction with needs being met is the ideal approach to enjoying this world.

advertisements and the media constantly spread the message of consumerism. Without question, it takes a very strong will to withstand these temptations, but if satisfaction (rather than indulgence) is a goal, then the appeal of these pleasures will certainly be reduced.

Desire for Kindness

"Forever will kindness be built." (Tehillim 89:3)

Ultimately, intent defines the value of a person's actions. Mundane activities can be elevated to the level of mitzvos when done with the appropriate objectives, and they can become sinful when done with the opposite intent. Thus, the pursuit of wealth may reflect unbridled desire for physicality, but it may also reflect the admirable goal of contributing to society. If a person feels a passion for kindliness, to give and do acts of charity, then it is appropriate to build wealth for this purpose. In this case, the drive for wealth is not motivated by a sense of selfish desire, but by the yearning to help others.[36] Of course, a person needs to ensure that his motivation is to help others and not just to increase his wealth.

> *A person needs to ensure that his motivation is to help others and not just to increase his wealth.*

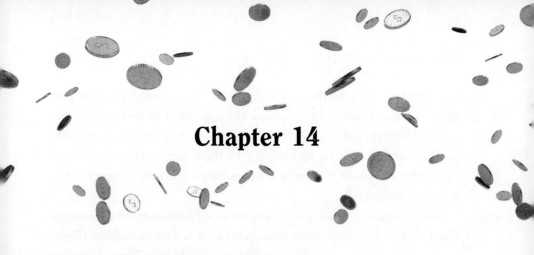

Chapter 14

Giving of One's Wealth

Although the Sages urge people not to be takers, they do encourage giving to those in need. This is a core value of the Torah. Aside from charitable giving, loans is another important form of extending help to others. Rambam presents eight levels of giving charity. Each level reflects a different way in which to give. The highest level is when the recipient is provided with the means to provide for himself so he will no longer be in need of others. The various levels of giving are focused on the relationship between the donor and the recipient.

An additional aspect of giving is its impact on the donor. How does giving and lending impact the giver in terms of his financial self-sufficiency and well-being? Lending has an additional dimension. It is a form of giving, but it is in the context of a legal relationship in which both the lender and borrower have obligations toward each other that are enforceable in court. This combination has ramifications as well.

Charity

"If there shall be a destitute person among you…
you shall open your hand to him…" (Devarim 15:7–8)

There is no doubt that giving charity and helping others is a central value of the Torah. One of the defining traits of the Jewish People is that they are *gomlei chassadim* (those who do acts of loving-kindness).[1]

This attribute reflects the benevolence and compassion that are part of our national fabric. At the same time, giving has an element that is obligatory as well. Indeed, the *halachah* teaches that there is a lien on the members of the community to contribute toward communal charitable obligations.[2] Charity is not simply a voluntary donation, but rather an obligation.

This obligation reflects a central tenet of the Torah that "...everything is from You, and from Your hand have we given to You" (*Divrei HaYamim I* 29:14). The Torah puts a lien

The obligation of giving charity reflects the belief that everything comes from G-d.

on property to teach that what belongs to man is really a loan from G-d. Consequently, man is limited in how he may use a small portion of his wealth since the lien obligates that this part must be used to help others. The Sages reiterated this concept in their statement: "Give to Him from His, for you and yours are His" (*Avos* 3:7).

Building Wealth through Giving

"There is one who scatters and gathers more." (Mishlei 11:24)

The Sages explain that the proverb, "There is one who scatters and gathers more," teaches that if a person gives charity, it will come back to him in even greater amounts, as the Torah states, "Because of this [charity], G-d will bless you" (*Devarim* 15:10). Thus, one who wishes to become wealthy should tithe.[3] Similarly the Sages said, "Just as salting food preserves it, giving to those who are in need will preserve wealth."[4] The opposite is true as well; one who withholds from giving in order to increase his wealth will find that he loses it instead.[5]

Why is it the "Divine law" that charity builds wealth? Why does one who performs this mitzvah also earn credits for his own success? The answer is provided in *Mishlei*, "One who is gracious to the poor has lent to G-d, and He will pay him his reward" (*Mishlei* 19:17). Thus, one who gives charity is rewarded both in this world and the next. With regard to this world, the Torah states that one effect of giving is "in order that G-d should bless you,"[6] where blessing implies success and good in this world. With respect to the next world, the verse concludes, "He will pay him his reward," implying a person will receive his reward in the next world.[7]

The ways of G-d do not always appear logical, but despite man's limited ability to understand them, they can be observed and even utilized.[8]

Giving charity provides the donor with reward in this world and the next.

Building wealth through giving charity is a manifestation of G-d's providence in this world, one of the hidden miracles that occur daily.

Extreme Giving

"Tithing is a protection for wealth." (Avos 3:13)

When Rambam asserts that the "middle path" is appropriate in nearly all areas of character development he refers to a healthy person who is not extreme in either direction. Sometimes, when a person is inclined to an extreme of a particular trait, the remedy is to go to the opposite end, temporarily, until balance is restored.

This applies in the realm of wealth as well. At times, a person may find that he is involved with his wealth, spending all his time pursing it or planning how to obtain it. He may be reluctant to give of it according to his means. Some might even be willing to cheat to obtain more and more. For others, their inclination toward attaining extreme wealth is reflected in the influence that wealth has on their behavior and decisions. The remedy for this is to move toward the other end of the spectrum. By giving excessive charity and gifts, a person will gradually move himself back to the "middle path." Once his "illness" is cured, he can return to more moderate

Giving away wealth is a way to protect it.

giving. By becoming a giver and realigning his beliefs around money, a person creates a protection for his wealth based on the principle that giving of wealth generates Divine protection of wealth. This principle operates not only when the problem is the lack of giving, but also when the issue is an unhealthy craving for wealth. Similarly, when a person has moved too far toward avarice, his unhealthy relationship with wealth can actually jeopardize it. Thus, the Sages say that charitable giving is a protection of wealth.[9] Charity is a remedy for this malady and therefore, paradoxically, it serves as a protection of wealth as well.

Limits on Giving

"One who gives should give no more than a fifth." (Kesuvos 50a)

Despite its fundamental value, the Sages placed limits on the extent of philanthropy. Although it is customary to tithe and give one-tenth of income to charity, a person should give no more than a fifth of his money away. The concern here is that if a person gives too much, then he may impoverish himself, putting himself in a situation where he himself would be in need of others. Clearly, benevolence that produces this outcome is undesirable.

Even giving must be done with wisdom. There are many considerations when giving charity, including priorities regarding who should receive,[10] which needs should or must be provided for,[11] and what method of giving should be used.[12] While most of the laws of charity focus on the receiver, the giver must also evaluate his own situation; his giving must be in accordance with his means. [13]

The source for this concept is found in the Torah itself. The Torah commands that a person should offer sacrifices on the festivals in accordance with his means "according to the blessing that the Lord your G-d gives you" (*Devarim* 16:17). While everyone has the same essential obligation, the wealthy must bring more than the poor. Similarly, when it comes to charity and other mitzvah donations, one should give in accordance with his means. The Torah is concerned about preserving man's financial means. Giving should never jeopardize financial self-sufficiency.

Thus, while the Sages teach that giving can increase wealth (see above, "Building Wealth through Giving"), this can only be done on a limited basis. Giving too much will not lead to increased fortunes, as this type of benevolence can be seen as asking for an "open miracle." In general, the Torah's approach to miracles is that man does his part without relying on miracles, and G-d takes care of the rest.[14] If man is going to give too much away, in effect he is expecting that G-d provide him with greater wealth without man doing his part. Charity can help increase wealth only when Providence can be viewed as hidden and man must look closely to see the hand of G-d.

Torah Precepts

"And by which he shall live..." (*Vayikra* 18:5)

The Torah commands to serve G-d with "all your strength."[15] Under certain conditions, this includes a person's obligation to part with his wealth in order to observe the laws of the Torah, and it may even entail giving up his life.[16] In particular, the Torah requires a person to give up all of his wealth in order to avoid transgressing a negative commandment.[17] At the same time, the Sages teach that a person is not required to give up all of his wealth in order to perform a positive mitzvah, such as purchasing the four species taken for the Sukkos festival.[18] Here the consensus of the latter rabbis is that a person is not obligated to spend more than a fifth of his wealth on a mitzvah.[19] Why are positive commandments different? If no monetary value can be attributed to mitzvos, as "all your desires cannot compare to it" (*Mishlei* 3:15), then should not positive commandments be treated in the same manner as prohibitions, and also require that a person give all of his wealth in order to fulfill a positive commandment?

As discussed previously, the Torah and the Sages emphasized the importance of avoiding poverty and dependence on others. Indeed, poverty is

> *The command to "live by them" relieves a person from spending excessive sums on positive commandments.*

even compared to death, and a person is certainly not required to gives his life in order to fulfill a positive commandment. The Torah commands that we "live by them," not die by them.[20] The commandments are to be a source of life and not the cause of death except under very extenuating circumstances. It follows that a person need not give up his wealth to fulfill a positive commandment, as this would leave him poor, the opposite of living by the mitzvos.[21] In a similar vein, the Sages set limitations on the amount that can be donated to the Temple.[22] The purpose of these limitations was to prevent people from putting themselves in a position in which they would be in need of others.[23] (See above, "Limits on Giving," for more on this point.)

Giving Gifts

"He who makes gifts to the rich,
it is only for a loss." (Mishlei 22:16)

The Torah teaches that resources must be used wisely; wasting a person's monetary resources is sinful (see above, "A Waste of Time and Energy," for more on this topic). Included in this category is the misappropriating of wealth by giving gifts to the wealthy. Such gifts are a misuse of funds that G-d has provided since they serve little or no purpose. Consequently, it is wasteful — or "for a loss." What may appear, on the outside, as a harmless gift, can actually be a sin.[24]

Material bounty is a blessing from G-d that requires responsible stewardship.

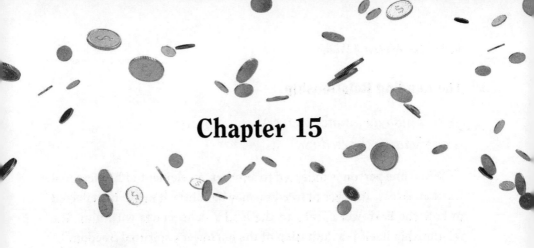

Chapter 15

Lending

*"When you lend money to My people...
do not act toward him as a creditor..."* (Shemos 22:24)

The Torah commands the lending of money to those in need. The Sages teach that the mitzvah of lending to someone in need is greater than the mitzvah of giving to the poor. The poor person is already in need and has experienced the embarrassment that comes with taking charity, while the person who is borrowing has yet to experience that feeling. The loan will hopefully enable him to get back on his feet and avoid being in need of others. It will prevent him from feeling shame.[1] Still, the lender is not obligated to destroy his own wealth through acts of kindness. A person is commanded to lend only when the borrower offers some sort of guarantee of the loan. Without collateral or a guarantor, there is no obligation to lend.[2]

> The command to lend is in effect when there is some form of guarantee for the loan.

The Lending Relationship

"A rich man dominates paupers, and a debtor is a servant to the creditor." (Mishlei 22:7)

When one person is indebted to another, an element of his personal freedom is lost. This loss of freedom may be subtle; it might be reflected in how the borrower speaks to the lender or interacts with him. The relationship itself is a limitation of the borrower's spiritual freedom.[3]

This servitude is reflected in the *halachah* as well. According to Jewish law, a lender has a lien on the borrower, known as *shi'bud*. Literally, this word means "bondage." The obligation of the borrower contains within it an element of servitude; in a sense, the lender now has a right in the borrower (for his money).

As a result of this arrangement, if the two parties disagree and find it necessary to go to court, the lender has the upper hand in determining which court should hear the case.[4] Similarly, in certain situations, the *halachah* tilts in favor of the lender in order to keep the pressure on the borrower to repay his loan.[5] Essentially, the borrower is in a more submissive position. In a legal sense, he is monetarily enslaved. By taking a loan, a person sacrifices his spiritual and financial freedom. Thus, even if a loan is not encumbered with the problem of interest, a borrower must still be careful that borrowing should not endanger his character or relationships.

Borrowing and lending affects not only the legal relationship between the two parties, but also the personal relationship.

Cosigning Loans

"A man who lacks [an understanding] heart will give his handshake to be a cosigner for his friend." (Mishlei 17:18)

While the Torah does command the lending of money to those in need, it does not obligate the cosigning of loans. Although the cosigner facilitates the loan, he is not directly providing for the person in need. In truth, the Torah and Sages dissuade a person from serving as a guarantor for a loan. Cosigning a loan when it is unclear whether the borrower will be able to pay (especially if the borrower is a stranger) is an act of foolishness, not kindness. If the borrower defaults on the loan, the guarantor will be drawn into a dispute in which he has no part. He will have to pay the lender against his will and will then be responsible to collect the debt from the borrower. He will experience strife due to money that did not bring him any benefit! Wealth is a gift from G-d to be administered wisely; in this scenario, the guarantor has acted irresponsibly with his money.[6]

Little compassion is offered for a person who acts in this manner: "Take the garment of one who cosigns for a stranger..." (*Mishlei* 20:16)! The guarantor's problems are of his own making; he unnecessarily placed himself in a difficult position. While there is sympathy for the borrower, as his life circumstances forced him into a situation where he needed to borrow, the guarantor was not compelled to make this choice.[7]

Shlomo Hamelech warns that a person can never know what will happen to his wealth. As a result, "a hater of handshakes will be secure" (*Mishlei* 11:15). Even when a cosigner is confident that the borrower will pay back the loan and he himself is ready to pay if necessary, there are no guarantees in life. While the guarantor may be prepared at the time he commits to help the borrower, his wealth may no longer be available when the time comes to fulfill his pledge. In guaranteeing a long-term loan, one puts too much trust in his wealth. It is therefore best to steer clear of cosigning loans.[8]

> *Cosigning a loan places the guarantor in a precarious situation without real benefit. In general, the Torah advises against playing this role.*

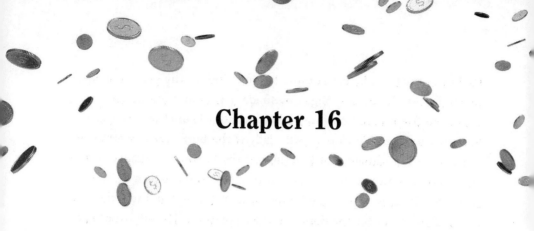

Chapter 16

Character Development and Money

One of the primary tasks of man in this world is to continually improve himself through the development of his character. Man is complicated; there are many aspects of his character that require refinement. Some traits relate directly to wealth, such as generosity and stinginess; other qualities, although not directly related to wealth, can also influence how a person acts around wealth. This next section will look at the interface between some aspects of general character development and wealth. It will also look at some features of society in general, that are relevant to wealth and character development.

Integrity

"You shall do what is right and good." (Devarim 6:18)

The Bible uses the term *yashar* to describe a person who is straight and upright in his dealings with other people. Such a person refrains from deceiving or misleading others and conducts his affairs with honesty and integrity.

Although integrity and uprightness are character traits that should pervade all aspects of a man's personality, they are particularly relevant in his monetary dealings. A person who lives his life in consonance with these traits will not change his approach in business out of concern that someone else may outmaneuver him and beat him to a deal; he is not looking for tricks or stratagems to outsmart his opponents. He similarly does not cast fear upon others in order to achieve his goals and he makes no attempt to advance himself at the expense of others.[1]

Uprightness goes beyond integrity in dealing with other people. It includes a concern for the general welfare of other people, even when they maintain a different philosophy or way of life. For this reason, the book of *Bereishis* is referred to as *Sefer HaYashar* (Book of the Upright), as it describes the lives of Avraham, Yitzchak, and Yaakov — people who epitomized upright conduct. The forefathers conducted themselves in this manner even when dealing with the people of Canaan, even though the Canaanite lifestyle was the antithesis of their own. Indeed, Avraham did not hesitate to pray for the preservation of Sodom, despite the wickedness that prevailed in that city.[2]

A person who does not conduct himself with honesty and integrity may think that he is advancing himself, but his behavior will ultimately catch up with him. The people he interacts with will perceive his crookedness and he will not succeed. Thus, "He who walks in innocence will walk securely, but the one who perverts his ways will be found out" (*Mishlei* 10:9). The monetary sphere, like other areas of personal interaction, demands a high level of moral character.

> *Integrity should permeate a person's conduct around wealth.*

Uprightness

"Better a little through righteousness than much produce without justice." (*Mishlei* 16:8)

The concepts of righteousness and justice are found throughout the Torah and form the foundation of any Torah-based society. In fact, they are the hallmarks of the descendants of Avraham: "For I know him, that he will command his children and household after him, and they will keep the way of the Lord, to do righteousness and justice" (*Bereishis* 18:19).

These core values must guide every action. Thus, *Mishlei* says it is better to maintain integrity and honesty than to achieve success through unethical means.

In addition to being the proper moral path, being upright also leads to practical results. The Talmud teaches, "If you want your wealth to last, plant an *adar* (tree)."[3] The *adar* reminds its owner of the *hadar* (the glory of G-d), constantly reminding him to conduct himself honestly and faithfully in his commercial dealings. If he does so, he can be sure that his wealth will remain with him. Conducting business in an honest manner is a means to preserve wealth. In fact, honest business practices can generate wealth as well: "If one wants to become wealthy, he should conduct himself faithfully."[4] Playing on the rhyme of the Hebrew words the Meiri states, "Straight and honest conduct, *yosher*, is a means to *osher* (wealth)."[5]

> *Honesty in business brings Divine blessing.*

There Are Consequences

"So is one who amasses wealth unjustly, in the middle of his days it will leave him." (Yirmeyah 17:11)

The ways of G-d are often unfathomable. The greatest of men have been vexed since antiquity by the question of how the wicked can often flourish while many righteous people suffer.[6] The prophet Yirmeyah reassures mankind, however, that if a person accumulates wealth in an unjust manner, he will eventually lose his wealth or he will pass on to the next world before his time, without enjoying it.[7] He is punished measure for measure; he wishes to accumulate wealth, even through illicit means, so his wealth is taken from him. His day of reckoning will come in this world, not only in the next.

State of Confusion

"A man of integrity will increase blessings, and one impatient to be rich will not be exonerated...One

*overeager for wealth has an evil eye; he does not know
that want may befall him."* (Mishlei 28:20, 22)

Nothing is inherently evil about wealth, but a person's approach to
it may be fraught with immorality. One who is overeager to achieve
wealth is described as *nivhal lahon,* literally, "hasty for wealth." Such
a person lives in a state of confusion, as his values are completely
skewed. As a result, he will do anything to achieve his goals, even if
it means cutting corners or acting unethically. One who desires to
achieve wealth quickly will likely end up stealing or hurting others.

Shlomo Hamelech emphasizes that such greed is punished measure
for measure; if one looks for unethical short cuts to wealth, "want may
befall him," meaning that his wealth will ulti-
mately disappear. In contrast, the "man of
faith" is honest in all of his dealings and conducts himself with integrity. He accumulates
his wealth slowly over time, but in the end,
his wealth is blessed by G-d, because it is acquired honestly as it says, "A
man of integrity will increase blessing."

> *Mind-set plays an
> important role in
> growing wealth.*

Self-Destruction

*"For the net seems spread out with free [bait], in the
eyes of every winged creature, but they wait in ambush
for their blood and lurk for their souls."* (Mishlei 1:17–18)

When a bird sees tasty bait, its only interest is the fleeting
pleasure it will derive from the food; the bird ignores the trap that
lies in wait which will bring a swift end to its desires. Similarly,
one who is overcome with the burning desire for wealth — one
who views the acquisition of wealth as a goal to be pursued for its
own sake — will ultimately be ensnared in a trap. While he may
enjoy the fleeting pleasure of profit, he very well may do so at the
expense of his soul, as he attempts to achieve his desires through
illicit means.[8]

Physical Rewards for Keeping the Torah

"I will provide your rains in their time, and the land will give its produce and the tree of the field will give its fruit...I will provide peace in the land, and you will lie down with none to frighten you..." (Vayikra 26:4–6)

If material wealth and success are not the ultimate goal and good for man, why does the Torah promise that the reward for proper behavior will be agricultural bounty, peace, health, and other physical blessings? Why, indeed, is earthly success a theme in the prayers instituted by the Sages?

Rambam explains that the blessings promised in the Torah are not to be understood as ends unto themselves. The purpose of agricultural blessing is not to enjoy the various fruits and to experience gastronomical pleasure. Nor is the purpose of peaceful times simply to live in the absence of war and strife.

The purpose of these blessings is to provide man with the opportunity to come close to G-d. When man must struggle to maintain his physical existence due to hunger, illness, or war, he is unable to focus his energies on serving G-d properly. While these matters are beyond the control of an individual, and a person is not doing anything wrong in preserving his physical existence, still war, famine, and the like prevent him from acquiring knowledge of G-d and performing His commandments. Thus, G-d promises these great blessings of health, tranquility, and bounty in order to provide the opportunity to serve Him in this world, so man may merit the ultimate reward in the next world.[9]

When physical needs are satisfied, it creates the space to achieve spiritual greatness.

This is the meaning of the Sages' statement that "the reward for a mitzvah is a mitzvah."[10] Service of G-d leads to more opportunities to serve Him. Man's ultimate purpose in this world is to achieve the World to Come, and this is accomplished best when his physical needs are provided for him.[11]

Honor

"He who shames his friend is a sinner; but praiseworthy is one who is gracious to the humble." (*Mishlei* 14:21)

One indication of the values of a particular society is the kind of people they honor. Most people see wealth as a measure of success and they therefore honor the wealthy, while the poor man, even if he has developed outstanding character traits, such as fear of G-d and humility, is lowly in the eyes of society and unworthy of respect. The Torah, in contrast, demands respect for those who perfect their character (among others), rather than for those who accumulate large fortunes.

A person who recognizes that the humble are deserving of respect is indeed praiseworthy, as he has distanced himself from the erroneous view of the masses and has inculcated proper values in himself. He is praiseworthy not only because he gives to them generously, but because he honors them; he realizes that wealth is not the true measure of success. In contrast, "He who shames his friend is a sinner." It is a sin to degrade somebody because he lacks wealth.[12]

> *The perfection of character is worthy of praise.*

Nonetheless, it is appropriate to honor philanthropists who use their wealth to benefit others and to spread the word of G-d. Honor is fitting for them not because they are wealthy, but because they use their wealth to help others. G-d entrusted them with the wealth and they use it properly — to serve Him. Although this is but a subtle difference, it conceptually reflects how a person values wealth.[13]

> *It is appropriate to honor those who use their wealth to help others.*

Appreciating What We Have

"He sent over his possessions." (*Bereishis* 32:24)

During his journey back to the land of Canaan, Yaakov crossed the Yabok River with his family and with all of his possessions. He then crossed back over to the other side. Why did he go back? The Sages teach that Yaakov crossed back over the river, thereby endangering himself, in order to retrieve some of his small vessels.[14] What was so significant about these small vessels that Yaakov felt compelled to retrieve them, even as he was fleeing from Eisav?

The righteous value all of their possessions, even those that might be viewed as insignificant. There are two reasons for this:

- Because they have their own things, they are less inclined to commit theft.[15]
- Protecting the assets they already have allows them to minimize the time they must work and prevents them from choosing inappropriate work.[16]

By freeing themselves from spending extra time in pursuit of material possessions, they have more time to concentrate on their spiritual goals.

For these reasons, Yaakov went to retrieve his vessels. Not because he valued these possessions in and of themselves, but rather because he valued the protection from sin and wasted time that they provided. The righteous care for their property, not because they love money, but because they recognize the blessing that G-d has provided for them and they desire to make the most of it.

> *Property and possessions can serve as a protection from sin.*

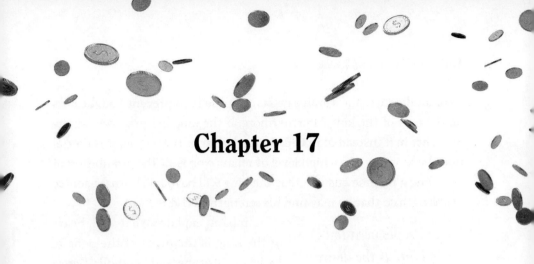

Chapter 17

Kings

"Neither shall he multiply silver and gold unto himself profusely." (Devarim 17:17)

A king must be wealthy in order to ensure his independence and to enable him to exert greater influence on his people. Indeed, because the needs of a king are greater than that of an average person, he must have significant funds at his disposal. Nevertheless, the Torah recognizes the danger that the king will go too far, taking advantage of his ability to levy taxes to grow his wealth without limit. The human desire for wealth is insatiable, and the king is in the best position to attempt to quench it.

The Torah therefore prohibits the Jewish king from amassing excessive personal wealth.[1] Rabbi Samson Raphael Hirsch notes that the Torah does not even offer a reason for this commandment, unlike the other laws of the king. No explanation is necessary; it is clear that avarice on the part of the king is destructive and undesirable.[2] Consequently, this is the sole occasion the Torah prohibits amassing wealth.

Other commentators suggest that the reason for this prohibition is actually mentioned in the Torah at the end of the section dealing with the laws of the king, as it is a catch-all for all of the king's special commandments. The Torah says its purpose is to prevent haughtiness on the part of the king.[3] Furthermore, if the king has great wealth, he will trust in it instead of in G-d. As the leader of the nation, it is crucial that the king develop a high level of reliance on G-d. The prohibition of amassing a fortune ensures that the king will have no alternate source of strength so that he may find his strength in G-d.[4]

> *People need to be vigilant, as the desire for money is insatiable.*

Rambam explains that the heart of the king is the heart of the people; he is a prototype and symbolic figure for the nation. When the Torah commands that the king observe certain commandments to elevate himself, the people should take note of the message these commandments convey. If the Torah limits the king's ability to amass wealth, then surely the people should be leery of this as well.[5]

Judges

"They shall judge the people at all times." (Shemos 18:22)

The Torah describes ideal judges as *anshei chayil* (men of means).[6] The Sages explain that this trait is critical; if the judges are financially self-sufficient, they will have no interest in bribes and flattery, and the integrity of the court will thus be upheld.[7] In addition, whereas a poor person lives in fear of the wealthy and powerful, a

> *Money and the desire for it can blur one's clarity of judgment.*

wealthy judge will not fear others and will therefore rule in accordance with his conscience.[8]

The Torah continues to describe judges as *sonei batza*, which can be understood to mean they "hate money."[9] While the judges certainly have money to take care of their needs and are financially self-sufficient, they are not interested in accumulating large sums of money. This helps protect the court from fraud because its judges will not be influenced by money.[10]

Peace in the Home

"He makes peace and creates all things." (Morning Prayers)

Peace is one of the greatest blessings that G-d can bestow upon man. In fact, the Sages instituted that the formal prayers conclude with a supplication for peace. Similarly, the three-part Priestly Blessing concludes with a blessing for peace,[11] and the Torah promises peace as a reward for observing its commandments.[12] Without peace, many of the other blessings are rendered of no value, as their advantage is only in the context of peace.[13]

One of the places where peace is most needed is in the home. Without peace in the home, the home becomes an unbearable place. Shlomo Hamelech reiterates this idea repeatedly: "Better a dry piece of bread with peace in it than a house full of contentious celebrations" (*Mishlei* 17:1), and "Better to dwell on a corner of a rooftop than [to dwell] with a contentious wife in a house of friends" (*Mishlei* 21:9).

One of the great sources of domestic strife is family finances.[14] In particular, severe poverty has the power to destroy a home. This is not a modern phenomenon; it is noted already in the Talmud: "A person should always be careful about having food in the home, as this is a common source of domestic quarrels."[15] If the basic necessities of the household are provided for, the chances for peace in the home increase. It is not great wealth that helps prevent family squabbles, but the avoidance of real poverty.

Marriage

"G-d said, 'It is not good that man be alone.'" (Bereishis 2:18)

The Talmud warns that a man should not marry a woman because of her wealth, going so far as to say that the children of such a union will lack good qualities.[16] While some limit the applicability of this statement to a situation in which the wealthy woman is actually prohibited to him based on her legal status,[17] others understand that this statement applies under all circumstances: One should never marry a woman for her wealth.[18] Even without a formal rabbinic prohibition against marrying for wealth, a marriage that depends on money is in danger of dissipating should the financial situation change. Marriage should be based on shared values, not people's net worth or on how much money each party brings to the marriage.[19]

The financial aspects of marriage cannot be ignored. A husband has monetary obligations to his wife that are outlined in the *kesubah* (marriage contract), and a woman has obliga-

Marriage should be based on shared values.

tions to her husband as well; still, they are not the purpose of marriage. A marriage must be based on values and shared purpose. Once this relationship is in place, husband and wife can set the economic foundation for their marriage. The monetary aspects of their relationship are practical and important, but are not its purpose.

At the same time, marriage can be a source of monetary blessing from G-d. One of the Sages would tell the people of his town, "honor your wives so that you may become rich" (*Bava Metzia* 59a). When Avram was compelled to descend to Egypt as a result of a famine in the land of Canaan, Pharaoh took his wife, Sarai, thinking that she was actually Avram's sister. The Torah then relates, "he treated Avram well for her sake" (*Bereishis* 12:16). On the simple level, the

Honoring one's wife can be a source of monetary blessing.

verse means that Pharaoh rewarded Avram with great riches because of Sarai. The Sages, however, interpret the verse as referring to G-d, not Pharaoh. Thus, it would read, "G-d treated Avram well for

the sake of Sarai." In other words, because of the honor that Avram gave to Sarai, G-d gave him this blessing. From here, the Sages derive the general rule that when a man honors his wife, it can lead to wealth. Blessing can only settle where respect thrives. While extreme poverty can lead to domestic disputes, honoring his spouse can bring a man wealth.

Friends

"All a pauper's brothers hate him; surely his friends withdraw from him." (Mishlei 19:7)

Both wealth and the lack thereof can be impediments to developing friendships. Wealth may foster haughtiness and brazenness, two qualities that certainly make it difficult to find friends, whereas a person with humility will find it easier to attract friendships and foster deep relationships. On the flip side, however, "The poor man is parted from his fellow" (*Mishlei* 19:4). A poor person lives in fear of others, as he requires their assistance to take care of his needs. His less-confident position forms a barrier between him and others. Furthermore, others, even his relatives, may be embarrassed to associate with him: "All a pauper's brothers hate him" (*Mishlei* 19:7). In contrast, "Wealth adds many friends" (*Mishlei* 19:4).

A person who is self-sufficient does not allow his wealth to foster haughtiness, and he is thus able to establish these relationships. "A man with friends is befriended" (*Mishlei* 18:24), as he has avoided the pitfalls that accompany both poverty and wealth.[20]

Shlomo Hamelech teaches that while friendships and personal relationships are not about money, money can — and does — play a role. Financial self-sufficiency is an important factor in developing healthy friendships, as it fosters conditions in which they can thrive.

Of course, a true friend will remain faithful despite any changes that occur in his friend's life, including his finances, as it says, "a friend's love is for all times" (*Mishlei* 17:17).[21]

Conclusion

The Torah's teachings in the area of wealth are part of the great repository of wisdom that can be found in the Torah. Rabbeinu Yonah explains in his commentary to *Mishlei* that one of the building blocks to becoming a servant of G-d is to seek and obtain wisdom.[1] But what is the purpose of obtaining wisdom? Why exert so much effort and sacrifice so much (as he explains is necessary) to obtain it? What benefit does it offer man? He answers that it says, "Then you will understand fear of G-d" (*Mishlei* 2:5). The purpose of wisdom is to obtain fear of G-d — which ultimately leads to understanding of G-d — as the end of the same verse says, "And you will find knowledge of G-d." Knowledge of G-d is the highest level in the fear of G-d, and wisdom is one of the building blocks to help one get there. Wisdom encompasses many different disciplines, but Rabbeinu Yonah teaches that the focus should be on obtaining fear of G-d — and ultimately understanding of G-d — as this is the true benefit to man.

In the area of wealth, like all areas of life, the Torah offers a great deal of insight. It provides wisdom, but ultimately with the appropriate intentions it opens the way to awe of G-d and understanding G-d. Reaching this level does not occur overnight. It is a journey and process. In fact, it is a process that extends over an entire lifetime, as there are always greater levels of wisdom available — and consequently a greater understanding of G-d — which is the pinnacle of man's achievement. There are a number of elements in this process, including obtaining wisdom, integrating it in one's life, and living in accordance with its teachings. All of these require time and contemplation.

Understanding money, wealth, and work is a part of the wisdom that leads to higher levels of fear of G-d. Indeed, the book of *Mishlei*, the classic Biblical book of wisdom and fear of G-d, is replete with teachings regarding "wealth," as has been seen throughout this book.

It is my hope that *The Wisdom of Wealth* has helped to clarify the basic concepts regarding money and wealth, and to dispel any misconceptions regarding these topics. In fact, this is one of the advantages of bringing together a wide range of topics that might appear to be unrelated. When similar concepts appear in different areas and sources, it is a sure sign that the concept is well-grounded and reflects truth. Together the various sources help bring clarity to the concepts at hand by providing a complete picture.

The Wisdom of Wealth has only scratched the surface of these topics; there remains a great deal to be uncovered and understood. It is my hope that this book will pique the reader's interest and encourage further discussion and in-depth study of these sources. Study provides the groundwork for thought and consideration about how the laws and values should be applied in the world of action. Aside from providing a path toward a course of action, there is an additional benefit that flows from the acquisition of wisdom when done with the proper intent. The more wisdom the individual obtains, the greater his opportunities for understanding G-d, which is the ultimate accomplishment for man, as the prophet states, "For only with this may one glorify himself — contemplating and knowing Me."

Notes

Introduction

1   *Perishus*, chap. 2 (translation by Daniel Haberman, *Duties of the Heart*, Feldheim Publishers, 1999).
2   *Avos* 1:17.

Part I: The Importance of Financial Self-Sufficiency

1   *Shabbos* 118a.

Chapter 1

1   Rabbeinu Yonah, *Avos* 2:2. See also *Tiferes Yisrael* 17 on this *mishnah*.
2   *Avos* 2:1.
3   Rabbeinu Bachya, *Kad VaKemach*, *Chemdah*.
4   Rambam, *Hilchos Matnas Aniyim*, 10:18.
5   See Rabbeinu Yonah, *Mishlei* 15:27. See also the *mishnah* at the end of *Pe'ah*, Rambam at the end of *Hilchos Zechiyah* and *Hilchos Matnas Aniyim*. See Rabbeinu Bachya, *Bereishis* 23:15, where he explains that Avraham did not want to accept a burial plot from Ephron as a gift because he disliked gifts, as is the way of the righteous.
6   Rabbi S.R. Hirsch, commentary to *Bereishis* 3:17.
7   *Berachos* 8a.
8   *Ein Yaakov, HaKosev Berachos* 8a.
9   Ibid.
10   *Chovos HaLevavos, Perishus*, chap. 5.

11 See *Nedarim* 7b and 64b, and Rashi, *Bereishis* 29:11.

12 See the comments of the Maharal, *Nesivos Olam*, *Nesiv HaOsher*, chap. 2, *Nesiv HaTorah*, chap. 4, and Gur Aryeh, *Bereishis* 29:11.

13 *Kiddushin* 30b with comments of Maharsha.

14 Interestingly, the Aramaic word for "skilled artisan" is *"chaiyusa,"* which comes from the root *"chai,"* meaning life.

15 *Eiruvin* 18b; Rashi on *Bereishis* 8:11.

16 See Ramban and Rabbeinu Bachya, *Bereishis* 8:11.

17 See *Anaf Yosef* to *Ein Yaakov*, *Eiruvin* 18b.

18 Rabbi S.R. Hirsch, commentary to *Bereishis* 8:11.

Chapter 2

1 See also Rambam, *Hilchos Shabbos* 30:7. There are factors that limit the application of this principle, see *Tur* and *Shulchan Aruch* 242.

2 *Yeshayah* 58:13.

3 *Beitzah* 15b.

4 *Aruch HaShulchan* 242: 44, *Sha'ar HaTzion* 242:12. See also *Beitzah* 15b, Tosfos, *"levu."*

5 *Yevamos* 63a with Rashi, ad loc., *"zavan."*

6 *Bava Basra* 110a.

7 See Meiri, *Bava Basra* 110a. See also Rabbeinu Yonah, *Mishlei* 12:9.

8 See *Mesilas Yesharim*, chap. 11.

9 *Shabbos* 114a; Rambam, *Hilchos Yesodei HaTorah* 5:11.

10 See Rashbam, *Bava Basra* 110a. See also the letter printed in the introduction to *Chiddushei HaGranat* (Rabbi Naphtali Tropp) p.26 (*Oraysah* 5749), stating that he was willing to become a farmer in the Holy Land in order to support himself.

There is an exception to this rule. If a person is a communal leader, then it is inappropriate for him to do work in public. Rashi (*Kiddushin* 70a) explains that it does not look good for the community if its leader does not have somebody to work for him, while Rambam explains that he will lose stature in their eyes. This exception is not based on scholarship, as it applies to any person appointed to a communal leadership position. See *Hilchos Sanhedrin* 25:4.

11   *Kesuvos* 110b; Rambam, *Hilchos Melachim* 5:12.

12   See *Chochmas Adam, Sha'ar Mishpatei HaAretz* 11:4; *Sdei Chemed*, vol. 5, Land of Israel #9, "Land of Israel," 9; *Avnei Nezer, Choshen Misphat* 95:8.

13   *Maalos HaMiddos-HaOsher.*

Chapter 3

1   Printed in the daily prayer book.

2   See Maharsha, *Sanhedrin* 108b.

3   See also comments of Rabbeinu Yonah, *Mishlei* 3:6, where he states that the entire Torah depends on trust in G-d.

4   See Ibn Ezra, *Devarim* 26:5; *Tur*, ibid.; Rabbeinu Bachya, ibid. See Rabbi S.R. Hirsch, who also takes this approach but translates *"oved"* as "going to ruin."

5   See Rashi, *Devarim* 11:6.

6   It is important to stress, however, that wealth ultimately only offers security if its purpose is understood correctly. Otherwise, wealth itself can cause man to be lost in the material world.

7   See *Devarim* 26.

8   *Bava Metzia* 33a.

9   See *Bava Metzia* 30b and *Shulchan Aruch Choshen Mishpat* 265 for details of these *halachos*.

10   See Rabbi S.R. Hirsch, *Devarim* 22:4.

11   *Bava Metzia* 33a with Rashi, ad loc. It is worth highlighting that the Sages viewed this change in circumstances as a punishment.

12   In a different context, see the comments of Rabbi S.R. Hirsch to *Vayikra* 14:34.

13   Gifts given as signs of endearment are not under discussion here.

14   *Hilchos Zechiyah* 12:17.

15   Ibid.

16   *Maggid Mishnah*, ad loc.

17   Rambam, commentary to *Avos* 4:5, and Maharsha, *Berachos* 10b.

18   *HaMaspik — Histapkus; Ein Yaakov* to *Berachos* 10b in the name of *Ahavas Eisan* and *Eitz Yosef*. See also *Chulin* 44b with Meiri's explanation of Rav Zeira.

19 See *Shmuel I* 9:7–8; see *HaMaspik — Histapkus* (last section) and *Nesivos Olam — Nesiv HaTorah*, chap. 11. See also *Yoreh De'ah* 246:21 in Rema and his explanation of *Kesuvos* 105b. His reasoning not to accept larger gifts from people seems to stem from the principle of "hating gifts."

20 See *Yoma* 71a and *Kesuvos* 105b.

21 *Avos* 2:2.

Chapter 4

1 See Meiri, *Berachos* 35b. Rav Saadia Gaon, *Emunos V'Deos* 10:14, reiterates the Talmud's conclusion, emphasizing that the only way in which Torah can endure is if the scholar supports himself. This is also clear in Responsa of the Rosh 15:8. Beis Yosef, *Yoreh De'ah* 246 and Shach, *Yoreh De'ah* 246:20, write that there may be times when this approach is not viable and Torah scholars must dedicate themselves entirely to their studies while others support them. When and where this applicable is beyond the scope of this work, but clearly there is a long-standing tradition to support communal rabbis with public funds. See for instance *Aruch HaShulchan, Yoreh De'ah* 246:39–40. See also later in this book, "So the Torah Should Not Be Forgotten."

2 Rashi, *Berachos* 35b.

3 *Avos* 3:17.

4 See *Tiferes Yisrael, Avos* 3:17.

5 See *Sanhedrin* 26b with Rashi and Tosfos, ad loc., "*machshavah.*"

6 Rabbeinu Yonah, *Mishlei* 4:24.

7 *Chovos HaLevavos, Perishus*, chap. 5.

8 Ibid.

9 It is interesting that Chasam Sofer (*Choshen Mishpat* 154), when discussing the topic of a rabbi receiving money from the community, noted that because of "our great sins" he did receive from the community and in a certain sense this disqualified him from discussing the question since it could influence his thoughts on it.

10 See Rema, *Yoreh De'ah* 246:21.

11   See Rabbi Ovadiah MiBartenura, *Avos* 1:15; Tosfos Yom Tov, *Avos* 2:2; *Berachos* 35b; *Hagos Maimoni, Hilchos Talmud Torah* 3:2.

12   See Rambam, *Hilchos Talmud Torah* 1:12. See also Chayei Adam, *Hilchos Talmud Torah* 10:3, who describes how even a working person who does not have much time to learn should study several hours at night. See also *Your Money or Your Life* by Vicki Robin & Joe Dominguez (Penguin Books 2008), pp. 198–199, for several sources that confirm that the typical work day prior to the Industrial Revolution was three hours.

13   See Rabbeinu Bachya, *Avos* 1:15.

14   Meiri, *Avos* 1:10; see also Horiyos 10b. See also Rav Yerucham Levovitz, *Daas Torah, Bereishis*, p. 106.

15   *Avos* 3:17.

16   Rabbeinu Yonah, *Avos* 3:17.

17   Rambam and Meiri, *Avos* 4:11. This is an example of reward or punishment measure for measure. Although at times it may appear to man that the dictum in this *mishnah* isn't operative, this is because there are many other factors that impact on reward an punishment. See *Tiferes Yisrael* 53 to this *mishnah*.

18   *Hilchos Talmud Torah* 3:6, 3:9–10.

19   Meiri, *Chulin* 105b.

20   *HaMaspik — Perishus.*

21   See *Igros Moshe, Orach Chaim* 111.

22   See Rambam, *Hilchos Talmud Torah*, chap. 3. According to Rambam, it would be appropriate to take time to provide for the most basic of needs if necessary.

23   *Avos* 6:4 and *Tiferes Yisrael*, ad loc.

24   *Alei Shor*, vol. 2, p. 612–614.

25   See *Taanis* 23a, *Yoma* 35b, *Berachos* 28a and *Gittin* 63b. See also *Chovos HaLevavos, Perishus*, chap. 5, and Rambam, *Hilchos Matnas Aniyim* 10:18.

26   See *Hilchos Talmud Torah* 1:9; *Chovos HaLevavos, Perishus*, chap. 5; *Avos D'Rabi Nosson* 6.

27   Rabbeinu Bachya, *Vayikra* 10:3.

28 Rabbeinu Bachya, Introduction to *Parshas Terumah* and *Avos* 4:10.

29 *Kesef Mishnah* on *Hilchos Talmud Torah* 3:3.

30 It should be noted that the first nineteenth-century *kollel* established in Kovna, Lithuania known as Kollel Perushim, was established with the purpose of producing future rabbinic leaders. This type of *kollel* perhaps could qualify under these guidelines by extension. True they were not yet in leadership positions, but they were training to be. This too could be viewed as a service to the community. The community itself would be taking responsibility for developing future leaders.

31 See *Igros Moshe, Yoreh De'ah* II 116.

32 See *Choshen Mishpat* 9:3.

33 For example, see *Igros Moshe* in *Yoreh De'ah* II 116, who clearly assumed this.

34 In general, the concepts and ideas taught by the Sages were for the larger body of the Jewish nation and form the normative approach. There can, however, be select individuals who operate their lives on a different level from most people (See *Berachos* 35b; *Biur Halachah* 156:*sofa*). Those individuals will operate with a different set of assumptions; for them this might not even be a conflict. The concepts presented here are for the majority of people.

Part II: Establishing and Maintaining Financial Self-Sufficiency

Chapter 5

1 Rambam, for example, does not cite it.

2 Rambam, *Hilchos Shabbos* 24:1, 5. See also Ramban, *Vayikra* 23:24.

3 See *Bamidbar*, chap. 35.

4 Rambam, *Hilchos Rotze'ach* 5:5–6. See also *Nimukei Yosef, Bava Basra* 144b (67b in the Rif).

5 *Bava Matzia* 30b with Rashi, ad loc. "*zeh beis*." See also Ramban, *Sefer HaMitzvos, Shoresh* 1.

6 See *Chovos HaLevavos, Bitachon*, chap. 3.

7 See *Tiferes Yisrael, Avos* 1:38.

8 *Meromei Sadeh, Berachos* 43b.

9   See *Ein Yaakov* in *Iyun Yaakov*, *Kiddushin* 82a.

10   See Sforno, *Koheles* 7:11.

11   Ben Yehoyada to *Arachin* 16b. He also suggests that parents will pray for the success of their children in their business.

12   *Sanhedrin* 24a.

13   Rashi, ad loc.

14   Rambam, *Hilchos Eidus* 10:4.

15   See Rambam, *Hilchos Ma'achalos Asuros* 8:17–18. Halachic authorities dispute whether this prohibition is Biblical or Rabbinic in origin. See Tosfos Yom Tov, *Shevi'is* 7:3, and Taz to *Yoreh De'ah* 117:1.

16   *Vayikra* 19:14.

17   Rambam, *Hilchos Rotze'ach* 12:12–14.

18   *Kiddushin* 82a.

19   Rambam, *Hilchos Issurei Biah* 22:13. In ancient times, studies were generally conducted in one-room schoolhouses, making the chances of being alone with a student's mother fairly likely.

20   *Kiddushin* 82a.

21   *Bitachon*, chap. 3. Also see sections in this book, *Buying Eternity* and *End of Work*.

22   See Rabbeinu Bachya, *Avos* 1:10.

23   Abarbanel, *Avos* 1:17. Don Yitzchak Abarbanel served the kings of Portugal and Spain during the fifteenth century.

Chapter 6

1   Rabbeinu Bachya and Tur, *Bereishis* 2:8; *Chovos HaLevavos*, *Bitachon*, chap. 3.

2   See Ibn Ezra and Sforno, *Bereishis* 2:15.

3   This touches on the question of G-d's knowledge and man's free will to choose his actions. See Rambam, *Hilchos Teshuvah*, chap. 5.

4   Rabbeinu Bachya to *Avos* 2:2 and also his introduction to his *Shulchan shel Arba*.

5   Indeed, the Meiri, *Avos* 2:12, explains the concept of doing a sin for the sake of Heaven as referring to performing mundane activities,

such as work, for an ultimate spiritual purpose. The use of the term "sin" for these activities indicates that it is a necessary evil.

6   See previous section, "Work and Creation."
7   See Abarbanel, Rabbeinu Bachya. See also Meiri on *Avos* 1:10.
8   See *Chovos HaLevavos, Bitachon,* chap. 3, and *Tiferes Yisrael, Avos* 1:38.
9   Rambam, *Hilchos Sechirus* 13:7.
10 Ibid.
11 Translation Rabbi S.R. Hirsch (Judaica Press).
12 *Tanchuma (Vayeitzei* 13).
13 Rambam, quoted by Rabbeinu Bachya, *Shemos* 20:9.
14 For example, *Chovos HaLevavos, Bitachon,* chap. 3.
15 Bartenura and Meiri (second approach), *Avos* 1:10; 2:2.
16 See Rabbeinu Yonah, *Avos* 2:2
17 *Avos D'Rabi Nosson* 11.
18 See comments of *Torah Temimah, Bereishis* 2:15, note 37.
19 Meiri, *Avos* 1:10.
20 See first approach in Meiri, *Avos* 1:10 and Rabbeinu Bachya 1:10.
21 This might also be true according to Rabbi Ovadia of Bartenura. He would have to understand that the *mishnah* which says to "love work" is speaking to a person who can't engage in full-time Torah study, thus he should work even if he doesn't need the income, while the *mishnah* which says both Torah and work are needed to prevent sin refers to a person who can engage in full-time study but doesn't have the financial independence to do so. Only then is it necessary for him to work.
22 *Mishlei* 12:11.
23 See Rabbeinu Yonah, *Mishlei* 12:11.
24 *Kesuvos* 59b.
25 Bartenura, Tosfos Yom Tov, and Meiri on *Avos* 1:10.
26 Radak, *Yeshayah* 5:11–12.
27 *Mishlei* 21:25–26.
28 Rabbeinu Yonah, *Mishlei* 21:25–26. Rabbeinu Yonah also notes that performance of the mitzvos requires energy and vigor, which the lazy person lacks.

29 See also *Chibur HaTeshuvah* 2:9, p. 440.
30 See Ramban, *Shemos* 20:8; *HaMaspik*, chap. 1, "The Ways of the Torah."
31 *Avos* 4:12.
32 *Avos* 2:5.
33 The Meiri, *Avos* 4:10, notes that man has a strong desire to amass wealth. This desire, in and of itself, can limit his capacity to absorb Torah. Thus, one purpose in limiting one's involvement in these activities is to help curb this burning desire.
34 Rambam writes that a great deal of man's ultimate reward relates to the degree of *de'ah*, knowledge, and understanding of G-d and His Torah. See *Hilchos Teshuvah*, 10:6.
35 *Eiruvin* 55a.
36 *Torah Temimah, Devarim* 30:13, note 15.
37 See Tosfos Yom Tov, *Avos* 2:5.
38 *HaMaspik — Bitachon.*
39 *Berachos* 35b.
40 *Chibur Teshuvah* 2:9, pp. 414–5. See also Rabbeinu Yonah, *Mishlei* 3:6.
41 Meiri to *Avos* 1:8 commenting on "make your Torah fixed."

Chapter 7

1 *Chulin* 84b.
2 Rashi and Meiri, ad loc.
3 See *Hilchos De'os* 5:10.
4 *Hilchos De'os* (ibid.) where Rambam writes for a man to "provide for his family according to his wealth."
5 *Chulin* 84b, See *Hilchos De'os* loc. cit., and *Hilchos Nashim* 15:19.
6 See *Chiddushei Ran, Shabbos,* 62b.
7 See *Hilchos De'os* loc. cit.; Meiri, *Chulin* 84a–b.
8 *Vayikra*, chap. 5.
9 *Sefer HaChinuch*, mitzvah 123. Some commentators disagree with the *Chinuch*'s application regarding this offering. See comments of *Minchas Chinuch* on this mitzvah.

10   Rashi, *Chulin* 84a.

11   Seemingly, Maharsha to *Shabbos* 140b offers a different explanation of Rav Pappa. See comments there of Rabbi Shmuel Shtrashun. The explanation here is borne out by the Meiri.

12   Meiri brings Rav Pappa's statement in his commentary indicating that either he did not have the rejection of the Talmud in his text or that at least the core idea is accepted (if not the application).

13   See *Shabbos* 140b with Meiri, ad loc.

14   Rashi, *Beitzah* 16a, "*kol mezonosav.*"

15   The Biur Halachah 529:1 notes that this was a problem in his time.

16   See Meiri and Rabbeinu Yonah, *Mishlei* 21:17, 20.

17   Rambam, *Hilchos Yom Tov* 6:20.

18   *Shulchan Aruch, Orach Chaim* 529:2.

19   Ibid., 529:1, and *Mishnah Berurah*, ad loc.12.

20   See Meiri to *Beitzah* 15b, who suggests that the principal of borrowing for Shabbos and Yom Tov is limited to the needs of *Kiddush*.

21   For example, see *Yeshayah* 22:12–15.

22   See Rabbeinu Yonah, *Mishlei* 21:17.

23   See also *Mishlei* 23:20–21 with comments of Rabbeinu Yonah and Rashi's comments to *Sanhedrin* 71, ad loc., "*ukraim.*"

24   Meiri, *Eiruvin* 65a. See also Rambam, Introduction to the *Avos*, chap. 5, who expresses this idea based on *Berachos* 57b.

25   See Rashi and Ibn Ezra, *Mishlei* 23:23.

26   See *Tur Orach Chaim* 155:1, where he says that a fixed time for Torah study should not be given up even if he stands to make a large gain.

27   Rabbeinu Yonah, *Mishlei* 23:23.

28   See *HaMaspik — Perishus.*

29   *Hilchos Teshuvah* 10:6.

30   *Devarim* 20:19.

31   Rabbeinu Yonah, *Sha'arei Teshuvah* 3:82. See *Sefer HaChinuch*, mitzvah 529; Rambam, *Hilchos Melachim* 6:8; *Sdei Chemed*, vol. 1, *beis*, for discussion regarding whether all forms of waste are part of the Biblical injunction or are rabbinic in origin. A *perutah* is the smallest copper coin in the Talmudic period.

32   Rabbeinu Yonah, *Mishlei* 18:9.

33   *Mesilas Yesharim, Perishus.*

34   Ibid.

35   *HaMaspik — Bitachon.* See also *Moreh Nevuchim* 3:12. See also *Mesilas Yesharim,* ibid.

Chapter 8

1   See Rashi and Meiri on this verse, *Sotah* 44a, and Rabbeinu Bachya, *Shemos* 31:18.

2   *Hilchos De'os* 5:11. It should be noted that commentators debate the order of the first two but all agree that marriage is the last stage, as this was the primary thrust of the guidance being offered.

3   Malbim, *Mishlei* 24:27.

4   Today we see many young people do not follow this order as they set out to build their own families. This is not a particularly modern phenomenon as the Chasam Sofer (1762–1839) already noted (*Orach Chaim* 156) that because of "our many sins" it is extremely difficult to follow the appropriate order as set down by these classical sources. Application to an individual's life will vary based on his own set of circumstances. For example, today it is reasonable to suggest if a person is studying a profession/trade, he is on the path to self-sufficiency, and this is thus adequate preparation prior to marriage, as the alternative would mean a very long delay before marrying. In general, a person would be best served by understanding and assimilating the principles and then seeking guidance where necessary as how to apply them to his situation.

In a similar vein, the Talmud has an additional level of interpretation of "Prepare your work outside and provide for yourself in the field; then build your house." It explains that the verse is referring to the study of Torah. Success in the study of Torah also requires that it be done in the correct order, and thus first *Mikra,* then Mishnah, and finally Gemara (*Sotah* 44a). Today, this is generally not followed in the exact manner recommended by the Sages. Here too, without question, in earlier generations when they were able to follow the correct order they achieved much greater levels of

Torah. Today, the student will certainly benefit by studying Torah in an order more closely aligned with the guidance of the Sages. While it might be impossible to follow the exact guidance of the Sages, the closer the student follows it the better off he will be.

5 *Tamid* 32a; *Avos* 2:9. It is interesting to note that according to *Avos*, the opposite of *"ro'eh es hanolad"* is failing to pay a loan. The borrower has failed to see beyond the period of the loan and to prepare accordingly.

6 *Berachos* 55a.

7 See Rabbi S.R. Hirsch, *Devarim* 29:8.

8 See *Shulchan Aruch, Yoreh De'ah* 249.

9 Meiri, *Kesuvos* 50a and *Bava Basra* 133b; *She'iltos* 64; See also Rabbi Akiva Eiger, *Yoreh De'ah* 249.

10 See also *Mishlei* 30:25.

11 *Niddah* 65a.

12 Maharsha, ibid.

13 See Meiri, *Mishlei* 6:6–8 and 31:25.

14 See *Igros Moshe, Orach Chaim* 2:111.

15 Ibid. See also *HaMaspik — Histapkus* on the advantages of not overworking.

16 *Hilchos De'os* 5:11. See Rabbeinu Yonah, *Mishlei* 21:17, where he describes how momentary enjoyment can impoverish. See above "Spending for Pleasure."

17 See *Yevamos* 63a with Meiri who implies that in general, owning buildings can lead to poverty.

18 See *Yevamos* 63a wherein the Talmud states that investing in a business is more lucrative than farming.

19 Another possible reason for the instruction to buy property is the possibility of growing produce for personal/familial consumption. See Maharsha, *Bava Metzia* 42a, based on *Yevamos* 63a.

Chapter 9

1 Rabbeinu Bachya, *Kad HaKemach, Chemdah*.

2 Rabbeinu Yonah, *Mishlei* 20:13.

3   See Meiri, *Mishlei* 27:23–27.

4   *Chulin* 91a.

5   *Chulin* 84b.

6   *Shulchan Aruch, Yoreh De'ah* 243:2.

7   Shach, *Yoreh De'ah* 243:7.

8   Meiri, *Tehillim* 128–129. See also *Chovos HaLevavos, Bitachon*, chap. 5; Rabbeinu Yonah *Mishlei* 3:5; *HaMaspik — Bitachon*.

9   *Tehillim* 20:8.

10 See Radak, ad loc.

11 See *Sefer HaChinuch* 546, Ramban to *Shabbos* 156b. See also *Igros Moshe, Orach Chaim* 2:111.

12 See Rabbi S.R. Hirsch, *Shemos* 16:2.

13 *Bereishis* 32.

14 *Bereishis Rabbah* 76:3.

Chapter 10

1   See Meiri, Ibn Ezra, Metzudas David on this verse; *HaMaspik — Bitachon*.

2   Ibn Ezra, *Tehillim* 127:2.

3   See comments of Meiri to *Tehillim* 128 that no wise man has disdain for making an effort and praise for indolence.

4   *HaMaspik — Bitachon*; Rabbeinu Bachya, *Kad HaKemach, Parnassah*.

5   See Rabbi S.R. Hirsch, *Shemos* 16:2. (Similar thought in section of "Emergency Fund" and "Trust" with this citation.)

6   Rabbi S.R. Hirsch, *Vayikra* 23:43.

7   Loc. cit.

8   Loc. cit.

9   Rashbam, *Vayikra* 23:43.

10 *Orchos Tzaddikim, Sha'ar HaSimchah*.

11 Meiri notes that G-d will help people who are able to put all of their trust in G-d so that they will gain more than their own human efforts could achieve on their own. This is an example of increased divine providence through cultivating trust in G-d. See earlier, "Building a Relationship with G-d."

12 See Rabbeinu Yonah on this verse.

13 Loc. cit.; see also Meiri, *Mishlei* 16:20 and Rabbeinu Bachya, *Kad Hakemach, R'shus* 5.

14 See *Mesilas Yesharim*, chap. 21. See earlier section, "Work and Creation," for other opinions on this point including *Chovos HaLevavos, Bitachon*, chap. 3.

15 See *Chovos HaLevavos, Bitachon*, chap. 3. See also *Ways of the Righteous*, Gate of Happiness.

16 This is apparent in *Chovos HaLevavos*, where it states that man was put in Gan Eden to work it; yet he still suggests that a person could reach a level where there would no longer be a need for the tests of work. Furthermore, his language is only that his livelihood will come without difficulty and effort, implying that he still must do something.

17 *Melachim I* 17:6.

18 *Mishlei* 30:12; *Hamaspik — Bitachon*.

19 *HaMaspik — Bitachon*; see also Rambam, *Hilchos Talmud Torah* 3:10.

20 Rambam, *Hilchos Zechiyah* 12:17; see also end of Taz to *Yoreh De'ah* 246:21.

Part III: Wealth and Poverty

1 *Bava Metzia* 33a; *Sanhedrin* 64b.

Chapter 11

1 Rabbeinu Yonah, *Mishlei* 18:23; see also *Sanhedrin* 81a, Rashi, ad loc., *"shelo neneh."*

2 *Bava Basra* 116a.

3 Maharal, ad loc.

4 18:23.

5 See Rabbeinu Yonah, *Mishlei* 18:23.

6 *Sanhedrin* 110a; Rashi, *Devarim* 11:6.

7 See *Sha'arei Teshuvah* 3:187–199 for extensive treatment of this topic.

8 *Sotah* 41b. The reference is to Herod Agrippa, the grandson of Herod the Great, who read from the Torah to the people during the

Sukkos after the seventh year of the sabbatical cycle. Although this is the king's obligation, Agrippa was technically disqualified from being the king.

9 Rabbeinu Bachya, *Kad HaKemach, Chanufah*.
10 *Sotah* 42a.
11 *Iyov* 13:16.
12 Rabbeinu Yonah, *Mishlei* 15:27 and 18:23. See also Rashi *to Shemos* 18:21.
13 *Mishlei* 10:15. See Rabbeinu Yonah on this verse.
14 See, for example, *Vayikra* 26:3–13.
15 *Bava Basra* 116a; see "Character Defect" above.
16 See commentary of Rabbi S.R. Hirsch, *Bereishis* 26:15.
17 *Shemos Rabbah* 31:14.
18 See Ben Yehoyada and *Ein Yaakov* to the *gemaros* in *Bava Basra* and *Chagigah*.
19 Rashbam, *Bava Basra* 116a; see also *Shabbos* 151b.
20 *Sanhedrin* 64b with Rashi, ad loc., "*lo*" and "*hasam*."

Chapter 12

1 Rabbeinu Yonah, *Mishlei* 10:16.
2 *Avos* 2:17.
3 Rambam, *Shemoneh Perakim* (introduction to *Avos*), end of chap. 5.
4 See Rabbi S.R. Hirsch's introduction to this psalm as well as his commentary on the entire psalm. As indicated in the text this psalm is crucial for understanding man's relationship to wealth and Rabbi Hirsch brings this out in his commentary.
5 *Bereishis Rabbah* 16:3; see Rabbeinu Bachya, *Kad HaKemach, Osher*.
6 *Bitachon*, chap. 3.
7 See Rabbi S.R. Hirsch on this verse.
8 See *Medrash Vayikra* 34:8.
9 *Divrei HaYamim II* 9:20.
10 *Melachim I* 10:27.
11 *Sanhedrin* 21b.
12 *Sanhedrin* 21b with Maharsha.

13 Rabbeinu Bachya, *Kad HaKemach, Osher*.

14 *Yirmeyah* 9:23 with Radak, ad loc.

15 *Kad HaKemach, Osher*. See also Rabbeinu Bachya, introduction to *Parshas Bo*.

16 Sforno, *Koheles* 9:3.

17 *Drashos HaRan* 6.

18 See Meiri to this verse; also Radak, *Sefer HaShorashim*, p. 78.

19 *Koheles* 5:12.

20 See Meiri, *Mishlei* 10:3.

21 See Sforno, *Koheles* 5:9–11.

22 *Avos* 4:1.

23 Abarbanel, ad loc.

24 128:2.

25 *Mishlei* 30:9.

26 See Ramban to *Devarim* 17:20.

27 Rabbeinu Yonah, *Mishlei* 19:1.

28 *Shemos* 20:17.

29 *Nedarim* 20a.

30 See *Torah Temimah*, *Shemos* 20:17, note100.

31 *Avos* 5:20. Gehinnom is a place of punishment for the wicked (otherwise known as purgatory) and Gan Eden is the celestial dwelling of the souls of the righteous.

32 See Rambam and Meiri, ad loc.

33 Rabbeinu Yonah on *Mishlei* 18:23.

34 See *Berachos* 57b, *Sotah* 49a, and *Shabbos* 118b.

35 Rabbeinu Yonah, *Mishlei* 19:1.

36 Vilna Gaon, *Mishlei* 4:13.

37 Rabbeinu Yonah, ibid.

38 Rabbeinu Bachya, *Kad HaKemach, Osher*; Rabbeinu Yonah, *Mishlei* 14:24.

39 Rabbeinu Bachya, *Kad HaKemach, Osher*; Rabbeinu Bachya, *Bamidbar* 32:2. See also *Medrash Tanchuma, Matos* 7.

40 *Ein Yaakov, HaKosev, Berachos* 33a.

Chapter 13

1   15:15.

2   Rabbeinu Yonah, *Avos* 4:1.

3   Ibid.

4   See comments of Sforno, *Koheles* 8:15, who also makes this point.

5   *Avos* 5:19.

6   Rambam, *Avos* 5:19.

7   *HaMaspik—Histapkus.*

8   Rambam, ad loc.

9   *Avos* 5:19. See also Vilna Gaon on this *mishnah.*

10   *HaMaspik*, ad loc.

11   See *Bamidbar*, chap. 24; *Avos* 5:22.

12   *Hilchos De'os* 1:4. See also 2:4 where he mentions some exceptions to this rule.

13   See Meiri, *Mishlei* 28:22 and *Avos* 5:19.

14   *Hilchos De'os* 1:4, 2:7.

15   *Chovos HaLevavos, Sha'ar HaAvodah*, chap. 4.

16   12:14.

17   *Chovos HaLevavos*, ibid. See also Ramban to *Vayikra* 19:2.

18   Ibid., who cites verses from *Bereishis*, chap. 1, as the source.

19   *Hilchos Teshuvah* 7:3. See also *Michtav Me'Eliyahu*, vol. II, p. 95, who writes that the desire for excessive pleasures is a sin in and of itself.

20   Similarly, if one takes less than he needs, his intent in doing so will define it as a positive or negative act.

21   *Bitachon*, chap. 4.

22   *Kiddushin* 29b.

23   *Bereishis* 30:30.

24   See Rabbeinu Bachya, *Bereishis* 28:20; *HaMaspik — Bitachon.*

25   Ibid., chap. 4.

26   *Ein Yaakov, Eitz Yosef, Chulin* 84a.

27   Maharsha, *Chulin* 84a.

28   Rabbeinu Yonah, *Mishlei* 16:26.

29   *HaMaspik — Perishus.*

30 Ibid.

31 *Mishlei* 23:5.

32 Rabbeinu Yonah and Meiri, *Mishlei* 23:4.

33 Ralbag, *Mishlei* 23:4.

34 *Yerushalmi Kiddushin* 4:12. (Translation from *The Path of the Just*, Feldheim, 3rd revised edition.)

35 See *Mesilas Yesharim, Perishus.*

36 Rabbeinu Yonah, *Mishlei* 19:6.

Chapter 14

1 *Yevamos* 79a.

2 *Bava Basra* 8b. This lien is similar to that found in the context of ordinary loan obligations.

3 *Ta'anis* 9a.

4 *Kesuvos* 66b and Rashi, ad loc.

5 Ibid.

6 *Devarim* 14:29.

7 See Rabbeinu Bachya, introductions to *Parshiyos Ve'eschanan* and *Ki Savo.*

8 See comments of Meiri to *Taanis* 9a regarding intent in using these principles.

9 *Avos* 3:13 with comments of Meiri.

10 See Rambam, *Hilchos Matnas Aniyim,* 8:15–18.

11 Ibid., 7:3.

12 Ibid., 10:7–14.

13 See Rambam, *Hilchos Arachin* 8:13.

14 See *Pesachim* 64b, Ramban to *Bereishis* 6:19, *Shabbos* 124a Rashi, ad loc., *m'shum.* See also Tosfos Yom Tov to *Demai* 1:1, ad loc. *HaChometz.* For additional sources on this topic, see earlier in this book, "Bitachon and Emergency Funds."

15 *Devarim* 6:5.

16 See Rashi, ad loc.; Sifrei, *Ve'Eschanan, piska* 7.

17 See *Yoreh De'ah* 157:1.

18 See *Bava Kama* 9b and Tosfos, ad loc., *"eliema."*

19 *Orach Chaim* 656.

20 See *Yoma* 85b.

21 See Raavad, *Bava Kama* 9b.

22 *Hilchos Arachin* 8:13; *Yoreh De'ah* 249:1.

23 It would follow that if a person is extremely wealthy, he may go over this limit, as he will not be in need of others even if he gives beyond twenty percent.

24 Rabbeinu Yonah to *Mishlei* 22:16.

Chapter 15

1 See *Shabbos* 63a, Rambam, *Hilchos Malveh V'loveh* 1:1, *Sefer HaChinuch*, mitzvah 66. It appears that the loan under discussion is not needed to pay an old debt, but rather to provide a basis to move forward.

2 Meiri, *Mishlei* 6:1, writes that there is no obligation to lend money without collateral; this ensures that the lender will be reimbursed. See also Tosfos, *Bava Metzia* 82b. This too is the simple reading of the *Mechilta Mishpatim Parshah* 19. Rabbi Y. Meir Kagan, in his work *Ahavas Chesed* (1:8), suggests a different understanding of the Mechilta based on his understanding of other sources. He takes the approach that the obligation to lend is even without collateral. Nonetheless, he says that the obligation is only to a person you know to be trustworthy and will pay back the loan. In this sense, both opinions agree that one isn't obligated to lend without some form of reliance that he will receive payment. They differ in whether the guarantee is in the form of physical collateral or personal reliability.

3 See Meiri and Rabbeinu Yonah, *Mishlei* 22:7.

4 See *Sanhedrin* 23a with Ran and also Rashba to *Bava Kama* 112b. See also *Shulchan Aruch, Choshen Mishpat* 14.

5 *Bava Basra* 171b with Rashbam, ad loc., "*eved.*"

6 Rabbeinu Yonah, *Mishlei* 17:18.

7 Ibid., *Mishlei* 20:16.

8 Ibid., *Mishlei* 22:26–7.

Chapter 16

1 Rabbeinu Yonah, *Mishlei* 10:9.

2 See *Ha'amek Davar* by Rabbi Yehuda Tzvi Berlin in his introduction to *Bereishis*.

3 *Beitzah* 15b with Meiri, see also Meiri, *Mishlei* 28:20. Another interpretation is that the Sages are referring to a well-known tree, which would serve as a way of identifying the property with the owner so that no one else could claim the land. The modern equivalent would be filing the appropriate papers with the local government to make sure that the land can legally be identified with the owner. If one has been blessed with property, he should take the appropriate steps to make sure it remains secure in his hands.

4 *Niddah* 70b.

5 Meiri to *Niddah* 70b. See also Rashbam, *Bava Basra* 89a, who brings this idea in the context of honesty in weights and measures.

6 The entire *Sefer Iyov* deals with this question. See also *Avos* 4:19.

7 Radak, *Yirmeyah* 17:11, see also *Koheles* 6:2 (although this verse does not refer specifically to ill-gotten gains).

8 Rabbeinu Bachya, introduction to *Parshas Bo*.

9 *Hilchos Teshuvah* 9:1, *Hilchos Melachim* 12:4–5.

10 *Avos* 4:2.

11 Rabbeinu Bachya, Introduction to *Parshas Bechukosai*.

12 Rabbeinu Yonah, *Mishlei* 14:21.

13 See *Eiruvin* 86a and Meiri, ad loc.

14 *Chulin* 91a.

15 Ibid.

16 Meiri, ad loc.

Chapter 17

1 The law limiting the king's fortune is limited to his personal fortune, not the government treasury. It is appropriate for the treasury to have money in order to accomplish legitimate governmental functions. When Rambam (*Hilchos Melachim* 3:4) says that the treasury may build up reserves, he refers to real wealth, such as gold and

silver. This should not be confused with contemporary governments' ability to create money (thereby deflating the value of the currency).

2 Rabbi S.R. Hirsch, *Devarim* 17:17.
3 *Devarim* 17:20. See *Sefer HaChinuch*, mitzvah 502; *Hilchos Melachim* 3:4.
4 Rabbeinu Bachya, *Devarim* 17:17.
5 See Ramban, *Devarim* 17:20, who writes similarly about the prohibition of haughtiness.
6 *Shemos* 18:21.
7 See Rashi, ad loc. See also *Sanhedrin* 7b, where the Sages state that a judge should be like a king who does not need anything. See Tosfos, ad loc., "*she'eino.*"
8 Rashbam, ad loc.
9 See Rambam, *Hilchos Sanhedrin* 2:7.
10 Ramban, *Shemos* 18:21.
11 *Bamidbar* 6:26.
12 *Vayikra* 26:6.
13 Rashi, ibid.
14 See "The Role of Money Arguments in Marriage," *Journal of Family and Economic Issues*, 2012, p. 1. Sonya L. Britt, Sandra J. Huston. Also see Dew, J. P., Britt, S., & Huston, S. J. (2012). "Examining the Relationship between Financial Issues and Divorce, Family Relations," 61, 615–628.
15 *Bava Metzia* 59a.
16 *Kiddushin* 70a.
17 *Shulchan Aruch, Even HaEzer* 2:1.
18 Ibid., Gra 6.
19 See Rabbeinu Bachya, *Bereishis* 24:3. See *Aruch HaShulchan, Even HaEzer* 2:1, for an alternate approach.
20 Rabbeinu Yonah on this verse. See also Rabbeinu Bachya in his introduction to *Parshas Tzav*.
21 Meiri 17:17.

Conclusion

1 2:1.

Bibliography

Abarbanel, D.Y. (1952): *Nachlas Avos*, New York: Huber Printing.

Bachya, b. A. (1993): *Rabbeinu Bachya on the Torah*, Jerusalem: Mosad Harav Kook

Bachya, b. Y. (1999): *Duties of the Heart*, Jerusalem/New York: Feldheim Publishers.

Bachya, b. Y. (1994): *Toras Chovos HaLevavos*, Jerusalem/New York: Feldheim Publishers.

Berlin, N.T. (1954): *Maromei Sadeh*, Jerusalem.

Danzig, A. (1991): *Chochmas Adam*, Jerusalem: Blum Publishing.

Danzig, A.: *Chaye Adam*, Jerusalem: Eshkol Publishing.

Dominquez, V.R. (2008): *Your Money or Your Life*, Penguin Books.

Eliyahu, Y.C. (1963): *Ben Yihoyada*, Jerusalem.

Epstein, B.H. (1903): *Torah Temimah*, Vilna: The Widow and Brothers Romm.

Epstein, Y.M. (1986): *Aruch Hashulchan, 8 Vols.*, New York: Wagshal.

Feinstein, M. (1959): *Igros Moshe, 7 vols.*, New York.

HaRambam, A. b. (2007): *HaMaspik L'ovdei HaShem*, Jerusalem: Feldheim Publishers.

Hirsch, S.R. (1989): *Commentary on the Pentateuch*, Gateshead: Judaica Press.

Hirsch, S.R. (1978): *The Hirsch Psalms*, Jerusalem/New York: Feldheim.

Hirsch, S.R. (2005): *The Hirsch Chumash*, Jerusalem/New York: Feldheim Publishers.

Israel Meir HaKohen, K. (1973): *Mishnah Berurah/Biur Halachah*, New York: Zundel Berman.

Levovitz, Y. (1976): *Daas Torah*, Jerusalem: Daas Torah Publications.

Lipschitz, I. (2004): *Tiferes Yisrael (Printed with Yachin and Boaz Mishnah)*, Vilna: The Widow and Brothers Romm.

Loew, Y. (1968): *Nesivos Olam*, New York: Judaica Press.

Luzatto, M.C. (1966): *The Path of the Just*, Jerusalem/New York: Feldheim Publishers.

Rambam, M.T. (1987): *Moreh Nevuchim*, Jerusalem: Mosad HaRav Kook.

Medini, C.C. (1961): *Sdei Chemed 10 Volumes*, New York: Friedman Publishers.

Meiri, M. b. (1970): *Commentary on Psalms*, Jerusalem: Makitsei Nirdamim.

Meiri, M. b. Z. (5729): *Commentary on Mishlei*, Jerusalem: Otzar Poskim Publishing.

Nachmanidies, M.E. (1958): *Commentary on the Torah*, Jerusalem: Mosad HaRav Kook.

Nisim, b. R. (1995): *Drashos Haran*, Mishor Publishing.

Trop, N. (1988): *Chidushei HaGranat*, Jerusalem: Oraysah.

Wolbe, S. (1987): *Alei Shor*, Jerusalem: Beis HaMusar.

Yaakov, B.S. (1988): *Ein Yaakov*, New York: Zundel Berman.

Yekusiel, Y.B. (1967): *Maalos Hamiddos*, Jerusalem: Eshkol Publishing.

Yonah, B. A. (1998): *Rabbi Yonah on Mishlei*, Jerusalem: Feldheim Publishers.

Yonah, B.A. (1967): *The Gates of Repentance*, Jerusalem/New York: Feldheim Publishers.

The following biblical translations were used in this work:

Artscroll Tanach

Hirsch Psalms

Koren Tanach

Pentateuch: Rabbi Samson Raphael Hirsch

Glossary

Anshei K'nesses HaGedolah: Men of the Great Assembly; an assembly of great scholars and the last of the biblical prophets during the end of the biblical period and the early Hellenistic period.

ayin tovah: A good eye.

ayin ra'ah: An evil eye.

bitachon: Trust.

chasidus: Piety; in particular, going beyond the strict letter of the law.

chametz: Leavened bread.

de'os: Attitudes or opinions.

derech eretz: Lit., the "way of the land." Also, a way of earning a living; general good behavior.

Gehinnom: A place in the next world where sinners are punished.

hadar: Glory.

halachos: Laws of the Torah.

histapkus: The quality of being satisfied with what a person has.

melachah: Labor, labors.

middah k'neged middah: Measure for measure.

mitzvah (mitzvos–pl.): A commandment, either biblical or rabbinic in origin.

perishus: Separation. In particular, separation from the physical world.

Sages: The rabbinic scholars of the Talmudic period; also used more broadly to include later scholars who followed in the traditions of the Talmudic scholars.

tzaddik: Righteous person.

yashar: Lit., straight; behavior that is honest and straightforward. An approach toward interaction with other people.

yishuvo shel olam: The continued development of society.

About the Author

Rabbi Chananel Herbsman graduated Yeshiva University *magna cum laude* with a degree in economics and received his *semichah* (rabbinic ordination) from RIETS. He has been working in the *kashrus* department of the Orthodox Union for many years. Rabbi Herbsman resides with his family in Upper Manhattan. This is his first book.